BEHIND THE SCENE

Born Amish, Raised Mennonite

A memoir

MARIANNE BONTRAGER

ISBN 978-1-68526-382-9 (Paperback)
ISBN 978-1-68526-383-6 (Digital)

Copyright © 2022 Marianne Bontrager
All rights reserved
First Edition

All rights reserved. No part of this publication may be reproduced, distributed, or transmitted in any form or by any means, including photocopying, recording, or other electronic or mechanical methods without the prior written permission of the publisher. For permission requests, solicit the publisher via the address below.

Covenant Books
11661 Hwy 707
Murrells Inlet, SC 29576
www.covenantbooks.com

INTRODUCTION

When I was born, my family was Amish. I respect my Amish heritage. My parents, whom I honor, moved on to join the Mennonite church and did the best they could to raise a large family. My intent in writing this book is for those of you who have suffered some form of childhood abuse as I did and that insight and peace comes to you as you read this story. Walk with me as my journey plays out, and hopefully it will give you tools to unlock any wounds in your heart on your journey toward healing.

I believe that this is prevalent enough among the Amish that leadership does not know what or how to deal with it. It has mainly been pushed under the carpet in secrecy for many. As for myself, it popped up in other unhealthy decisions I made because of the "no talk" rule.

In my case, it was such a shameful, dark secret that I could not talk about it to anyone. Later in adulthood, it played out in decisions that I made and the choices even in the type of a marriage partner whom I chose.

I did not write this book because I have achieved great success. I wrote it because one day I was walking on the beach, attempting to clear my head. I was in search of answers of the many seemingly difficult things that I was facing. Something very unusual happened to me. I heard an audible voice behind my right shoulder say, "I want you to write a book to the Amish." Startled, surprised, and mystified,

I immediately turned around to see who spoke, and there was no one around. I knew I was not crazy because I do not hear voices.

In my mind, sometimes I would have a conversation with that voice suggesting to it that I was never Amish, even though my parents were when I was born; but I knew my story was. Another dilemma was my writing skills. As a registered nurse, we were taught to abbreviate and shorten our sentences. That does not make a good story.

One day as I was attending a workshop on writing, I sat down with a successful author who told me to discard everything I had written to date and start over. I thought I was close to completing it. She said, "You are talking about your book like it is another person. You are not owning your own story." I went back to do more heart searching. It has taken me awhile to face what it was like. The influence growing up stays hidden unless my heart can open for God to replace it with something better.

My heart is filled with gratitude for two of my friends, Sharon Tracy and my childhood friend whom I called Ann in the story, who have helped me put my thoughts on paper. I am also thankful for my husband who supported me. My prayer is that the reader of this book can heal from shame and be able to know how much you are loved by God. Christ came to heal the brokenhearted.

Being the author of this book, I questioned whether I should disclose my real name. It is a true story of what I experienced; however, my wish is not to embarrass or harm the children of my brothers and sister or their children who have no idea that their parents were a part of this sexual abuse. I do not feel it is fair for them to bear the responsibility or shame from friends or the community for the sins of their parents, aunts, or uncles. The Amish and Mennonites have great memories and know the genealogy of people in their community. For that reason, I choose to protect them.

CHAPTER 1

Traveling through the busy airport at Dallas, I was on a layover, waiting for my next flight home. As I was people-watching, I noticed a few rows over a group of girls chatting amongst themselves. They looked different. They reminded me of a similar group of girls I observed a year earlier at a museum in Washington D. C. Shy and keeping to themselves, they moved quickly from one exhibit to another, speaking softly to each other, not making eye contact with me or the public. I could feel their awareness of themselves, recoiling from the scrutiny of being looked at as being different.

My next move was to have a conversation with the girls at the Dallas airport. What was their mission? Were they on their way to it, or were they returning home? Were they possibly attending the same Bible school I once attended? Where was home? With reluctance, they timidly said they were volunteering at a nursing home for a short time. It was clear they were not interested in engaging in a conversation, even though I divulged that I was once a part of their story.

Amish or Mennonites, who are we, and where did we come from? What is the difference between Amish and Mennonites? And why do we believe what we do?

Allow me to share some history. In the 1500s, Europe with its caste system started changing when the printing press was invented. People began to gather in small secret groups to read the Bible. Even the lower-class peasants were learning to read (who by the way, dressed much the same as the Amish do today, as well as some sects of Mennonites). Only a century earlier, reading the Bible was punishable by death by the Roman Catholic Church.

Numerous leaders in the Catholic Church began questioning the practices of the state-run church. Martin Luther, a German professor of theology, also a monk and priest, emerged in the sixteenth century. He questioned indulgences placed on the people by the Catholic Church. An indulgence is the amount of punishment one had to undergo for their sins. This also had monetary attachments to it that were cooked up in secret by the hierarchy of the Roman Catholic Church. "It's salvation through faith, not works," he proclaimed and "justification by faith." He also wanted people to want to go to church, but not because they were forced. He set about to challenge the power of the pope and the Roman Catholic Church doctrines.

Luther still believed in infant baptism. It was the initiation of the child into the state census. This gave control to the Roman Catholic Church, which was the ruling government of the state, plus the religion. This influenced the peasants. He encouraged the people to stay a part of the church. He was hoping the Roman Catholic Church would see the error in their manipulating doctrines and implement the changes he was proposing in his writings. But the Catholic Church rejected his writings, and as he stated, "Kicked him out." In spite of him being persecuted by the Catholic Church, Luther later persecuted those who did not go along with his teaching.

Zwingli, a Swiss Catholic priest, an Anabaptist and Greek scholar was known as a Reformer who started the Protestant movement. He wrote sixty-seven articles, hating indulgences and images in place of worship, promoted clerical marriage and translated the Bible from Greek to German.

In 1523, in Zurich Switzerland, this group of people called Anabaptists broke from both Luther and the Roman Catholic ranks. They refused to submit to Martin Luther as well as the hierarchy of the Catholic Church. To this day, they refuse to have a hierarchy amongst themselves. People referred to them as "social revolutionists." Others called them the "radical reformers." They declared that they had left the Roman Catholic Church. This is what is known today as the Reformation.

BEHIND THE SCENE

Martin Luther was rejected by both the Catholic Church and the Anabaptists. He was forced to go into hiding for fear of his life. During that time, he completed the translation of the Bible from Latin to German.

And so it was in 1536 that a man named Menno Simons, who was a Dutch Catholic priest from Zurich, Switzerland, joined the Anabaptist movement. He soon advanced in the ranks to become a strong voice and leader. He also was not intent on staying a part of the state-ran Roman Catholic church. Baptism is when a child is capable of understanding and experiencing salvation, he believed.

The Anabaptists went about baptizing converts and fell in love with Christ as the center of their life. The Bible was there to confirm Christ. They were given the name Anabaptists by outsiders because they were baptizing a second time. The state-ran government of the Roman Catholic Church went about killing them for their outright crime. Many fled, went into hiding, and if caught were put to death by torture, most often by drowning. State officials would bind them hands and feet and throw them in a lake. Some statesmen would declare, "There's your second baptism, if that's what you want!"

They were persecuted and killed mercilessly, living in constant fear, wondering when the Roman officials would come knocking on the door, seeking to eliminate any Anabaptists in the house.

Menno persisted to challenge the control of the pope by teaching on numerous differences that he saw from the Bible. He wrote seven ordinances for his group, which he stated replaced the sacraments of the Roman Catholic Church.

To this day, I have benefitted from the persecution that my forefathers went through. My church also referred to them as Ordinances. At the age of twelve, these same ordinances were taught to me in what is called instruction class. This allowed me to join the church and be baptized.

The ordinances are the following:

1. *Baptism with water.* On the front row of the church, we as new believers were ushered in. There with a few of my friends, I publicly confessed my faith as a Christian, show-

ing my intent to follow the ordinances of the Church. From a cup of water, the minister poured a small amount on each of our heads, saying, "I baptize you in the name of the Father, the Son, and the Holy Ghost."
2. *Communion.* This is celebrating the body and blood of Christ. We did this twice a year. We combined foot washing and communion. Communion was bread and grape juice.
3. *Foot washing.* This teaching is taken from the time Christ took communion and washed his disciple's feet. Growing up, the women and men always sat on separate sides of the church. For foot washing, tubs of water and towels were brought into the church. After washing the other person's feet, we would stand, shake hands, and then kiss each other with a holy kiss on the cheek.
4. *Holy Kiss.* They kiss each other with a holy kiss on the cheek. We did not do this routinely when greeting each other. Only after foot washing.
5. *Anointing with oil.* This was done primarily by deacons or ministers when someone was sick or on special occasions.
6. *The head veiling or "covering."* The head covering is for the women. Some of the Mennonite churches in different areas have the ordination of ministers instead of the head covering.
7. *Marriage.* Is to be honored between a man and a woman.

In the seventeenth century in Europe, a disagreement came up in the movement. A man named Jakob Ammon, a Mennonite bishop, was convinced that Menno was becoming lax in his discipline toward his followers. Followers of Menno Simons were called Mennonites by that time. Ammon believed Menno needed to excommunicate people for not adhering to the rules. He wanted the group to be stricter. He left the Simons group to start his own. They became known as Amish.

When excommunication is implemented in the Amish church, it is the highest form of discipline. They give that person over to

BEHIND THE SCENE

Satan. This is taken from the Bible in verses like, *"Whom I have delivered unto Satan, that they may learn not to blaspheme"* (1 Timothy 1:20 KJV). The group would then shun the excommunicated one by not having any fellowship or business dealings with them. They hoped they would see the error of their ways, repent, and return to the fellowship.

Unlike Ammon, Menno Simons believed that discipline within his movement was meant to confront, by discussing misconduct. If this error persisted, that person is then put out of fellowship from the group by excommunication. This to Menno was a better way than to first excommunicate people or put people to death for misconduct as was the custom of the Roman Catholic Church, which was also the ruling state government. When a baby was baptized, they became a part of the state census.

Another area of nonconforming was their refusal to serve in the military. Especially if during a war it would require killing another individual, they refused to comply. Their desire was to resolve conflict between warring factions.

My mother told me when the Amish and Mennonites were drafted to go to war, they were deployed to various military training camps. They refused to pick up a gun to kill. Their statement was, "You can kill me, but you cannot force me to kill." Adjustments were made by the US and Canadian governments. They served the same amount of time as the military working in hospitals and other areas of service approved by the government. Pegged as "pacifists," they became known as "conscientious objectors."

To date, the Amish are seen in their desire to live separately from society. By modesty and by their works, they profess salvation. They believe God decides whether they go to heaven by weighing their obedience to the rules of the church as the bishop and preachers interpret the Bible. As a result, it is very difficult for them to have assurance of their salvation. With the insecurity of salvation, they fear God is watching with His eraser, ready to blot out their name from the book of life.

They Amish do not believe in owning cars, computers, phones, or radios, which keeps them off the grid. The Amish continue to travel with their horses and buggies. Practicing humility motivates almost everything they do. Evangelism was once a large part of the movement, but over the years, seeking converts and spreading the gospel is less of a priority to the point that it is not done today.

The Amish church services are held on Sundays. Twice a month they get together in various homes. The backless benches where they sit for services travel in a carriage from home to home for a period of time for these meetings. On Sunday mornings, the minister usually opens with singing, which is followed by all taken from the High German song book in a Gregorian type singsong style.

Traditionally the Bible is read in High German from Bibles, which are kept with the church belongings and passed out on Sunday mornings. High German or Old German as they call it, is not usually taught at home or in their schools. Children, teens, and sometimes newly ordained ministers (which are ordained by lot) have difficulty understanding or reading the Bible in High German, so it is mostly not understood nor read at home. The doctrines have been passed down verbally by ministers and reinforced by parents for generations often without the understanding or the meaning from scripture.

The Amish learn English in school, which they speak in public. I did not learn English fluently until I was six in preparation for school. The Amish and some Mennonites speak a different dialect of German amongst themselves, which comes from Switzerland and Southern Germany. It is referred to as Pennsylvania Dutch. There has not been a translation of the Bible into Pennsylvania Dutch yet, which could encourage the Amish to understand the Bible by reading it.

Reading an English Bible is not encouraged today, nor do they carry a German or English Bible to church. This sadly does not allow open discussion or for the Bible to be an avenue to explore who God is to experience salvation. Is this why evangelism is not done today? I find it interesting when the Mennonites and Amish left the Catholic Church during the Reformation, it was because they read the Bible. They understood that Catholics were not adhering to the teachings of it. Or is it because they were looking to flee from the persecution, in which they made an agreement to be silent about their faith? A province of France called Alsace needed farmers to work the land. France opened the doors to the Anabaptist Amish to settle there, if sadly they would agree not to evangelize.

I have watched Amish teens do their *Rumspringa*. Salvation by a relationship with Christ is frequently not real to them. Rumspringa is around mid-to-late teens where parents and the church turn a blind eye to allow the teens to "sow their wild oats" before they settle down. Saturday evenings finds teens getting together for what is called a hymn singing. They gather at the farmhouse where the Sunday-morning services are held. At the singing, they file into the house with the girls separated from the boys and sing mostly in English out of a hymnal. Afterward, it adjourns most of them go to the barn where they experiment with things forbidden by the church, such as musical instruments like guitars or harmonicas. Harmonicas are tolerated after joining the church but not condoned within the church. Worldly dress is experimented with. They frequently indulge in drinking alcohol and even smoking. A few have been so wild as to purchase a car, which to the leadership of the church puts them in real jeopardy of going to hell. This can go on for years. It varies with each person. When they are ready to settle down and have "sown their wild oats," they then join the Amish church as a member. This is also a time when they can lose young people out of the organization to what they call "the world."

I think during the time when young people are free to "sow their wild oats," before joining the church, young people can get into all kinds of activities that are confusing. Boundaries are dim to nonexistent. The rules change from "you cannot" to "let me try this out." They feel free of the restraint that the rules of the church have put on them, and for the first time, their choices have no boundaries. The restraints are taken off. Growing up, they are not familiar with living without rules, so the opportunity to choose is exhilarating. They may feel shame but are free to indulge. This can go on for years. It varies with each person.

This is a precarious time should they choose not to join the church and go out into the world. Many do return when they are ready to settle down and have "sown their wild oats" or found a mate. They cannot get married until they put aside all their wayward activities and become baptized, which makes them a member of the church. It is what they are familiar with and where their families and friends are. They then join the Amish church as a member and put all these activities aside. If they have a car, they are required to sell it before joining the church.

The Amish held much in common with us as Mennonites. Separation and isolating themselves from the state and society is a key belief. We were taught secular culture would pollute our ways with its pride, greed, materialism, and immorality. Our salvation is through obedience. This separateness not only isolates us from the world, but also to ourselves by creating a wall around us because of our beliefs. I found pride in our separateness, especially because we believed we had the truth. This separateness in obedience to the church held me under the umbrella of control to the rules by submission.

One day when I was talking to my cousin, who was born Amish and who is now Beachy Amish, a more conservative church than the Mennonite church, shared her concerns. She said, "The Amish speak Pennsylvania Dutch. In their church services, they sing and read the Bible in the High German. Children are not taught to speak or rarely read High German in their schools, so they do not understand it. When young people stray, they have no foundation in the Bible or relationship to it. How could they? They have only the rules of the church told to them by their parents and ministers. The rules are easily discarded, and they mean nothing to them. God is not real to them."

CHAPTER 2

I was born into an Amish family. We lived in a small Midwest community where my parents struggled to survive. Dad's daytime job was shoeing horses for the Amish. He learned the trade from his father on the family farm. Moving our family within the Amish community was frequent. We moved to a different house to rent every year. On one of those moves, we lived on Grandpa's farm for a year. The big house was ours, and Grandma and Grandpa lived in the "dawdy" house. That is how many Amish families care for their elderly parents—by building a small house on the family farm instead of sending them to a nursing home. Mom told me that Grandma (her mother-in-law, Mary) instructed her on many occasions with advice she did not ask for in disciplining her children. She was quite verbal and disapproving of the way Mom did not keep up on housekeeping and chores. With so much work and little ones active underfoot, there was a lot of cruel criticism and hurt to wound her heart.

Grandpa was a disciplinarian, unforgiving, giving us a stern look of disdain centered around the rules of the Amish religion. Any weakness in me or my siblings initiated scorn.

I remember him sitting on his rocking chair in the corner reading the Bible, quoting scriptures at us. He said if they were not followed, we would go to hell. It was the discipline of the fear of going to hell if we were not obedient. One of the things he'd say was, "*Spare the rod and spoil the child*," from the Bible (Proverbs 13:24 KJV). Somehow, I felt like there was something wrong with me. I didn't know what, but deep down, I felt like I was bad. We were afraid of him.

I saw grandpa function by a strong hand of control as the head of his family. It was a pattern I recognized later in a few other pious men who were appointed to leadership positions in the church or a husband to his family. The wife and children fell into lockstep behind dad, as they attempted to follow his demands. His criticism and uncontrolled anger could easily escalate to rage, which he believed he was entitled to because of his position. Instead of him changing, he insisted that his family change. He was unaware that kindness and love are the keys to change one's heart.

I'm told restrictive discipline and severe beatings were frequent for Dad as a young child and into his teen years. Other siblings confirmed this. His brothers also misbehaved but with no consequence. Insecurity, betrayal, self-hatred, and low self-worth were his constant companions. He felt rejected, hurt, and angry but was forbidden to show his anger or talk about it, so he swallowed it. Not a word did he dare to say. After all, is not anger a sin in the church? How could he know that the Heavenly Father is a loving Father who wanted and loved him? He could never follow the rules of the church perfectly enough to be accepted.

The Bible says to be angry and sin not. I believe anger can be your strength. Little did he know it's okay to be angry when a wrong is committed against yourself or anyone. He thought God was an unloving disciplinarian, who would send him to hell for doing or thinking anything that was not in line with his father or the church. Why would he want to follow such a God?

To me, anger turned inward, condemning yourself, puts you face-to-face with depression and sadness. It's a process of denying yourself, not knowing or approving of who you are. When the Bible mentions that we need to deny ourselves, I see that as preferring and honoring another person, bringing out the best in them but not losing who I am. Dad did not experience Christ's love. Dad became silent and sullen holding on to grudges, taking out his frustrations sexually.

BEHIND THE SCENE

Mom, born in Kansas, was the firstborn of her father's second marriage. His first wife died during childbirth and left him with four children. He later moved his family to Wisconsin. There, Mom attended school until sixth grade, which was all the state required. She loved school but was needed to help with the work on the farm and the five younger siblings that came along. She also loved to read and spell which, as she got older, kept her educated well beyond the sixth grade. As a child, she was valued for her work habits. That is still valued in children today with the Amish.

She told me of an incident when she was a young girl. She questioned why she could not wear beautiful floral dresses. God dressed the flowers so beautifully. Why could she not wear splashes of color to be as beautiful as them. Her mom and dad saw this as a step into worldliness and pride. She could not be extravagant in her dress. Her dad was very strict, demanding obedience from her to follow the rules of the church. Her mom was more loving, she said, but her role was submission to her dad's decisions. She could not confront him even if she did not agree.

She confided in me that before she and my dad were married, she couldn't wait to get away from home, even though she questioned whether my dad was the right one for her to marry. If she married, she would no longer be subject to her parents' demands that she work away from home for outside families. It was hard work, and she was tired as she struggled.

As a hired maid caring for large families on their farms, she was washing diapers daily in a pail of water before adding it to the rest of the laundry load, cleaning house, caring for siblings, or working in the garden, canning, and doing chores. Then there was milking cows. The milk was put through a separator, which separated the milk from the cream. After the milk was separated, there was the tearing apart of the separator. Washing the separator was heavy and cumbersome. Then there was cooking and doing dishes. At the end of the week, her wages were paid to her parents.

Her sister Lydia, just younger than Mom, worked for their "English" neighbors. (The English are referred to as people outside the Amish Church). Her eyesight was poor. She wore thick glasses.

(Her youngest sister Sadie also had this ailment). The Amish bishops talked about her handicap and, at the "English" neighbor's suggestions, agreed to have her go to the closest city to learn the skills of a nurse's assistant. Word came back that she was straying from the Amish faith, especially in her dress. The Amish bishop and some of his followers went to where she was living to pray with her and check up on her. As they were praying with closed eyes, the bishop peeked at her. She told my mom later, "He was checking on my sincerity!" This suspicion greatly irritated her and drove her to seek other options.

Lydia's neighbors, who were helping her find her way, assisted her in her next decision. She decided to go to Africa as a Baptist missionary, thereby leaving the Amish. This brought shame on the family. She now dressed like the world, modestly but worldly. After all, her dress had been a part of her being separate from the world.

Mom went on to say that marrying my dad was not the only reason she wanted to leave home. In our conversation as adults, this was a very painful memory filled with shame and secrecy. Her older half brother would come into her room at night, get into bed with her where she was sleeping with her sister, and there he would have his way with her sexually. This was a routine occurrence.

I asked her if she ever told anyone. She said yes, but when she told her mom, her mom said, "You must have done something to bring that on to make him do that." This put the blame and shame back on her, and she had no one to confide in who would confront his misconduct. Her sister told her in disgust that she was glad it was not her. My question is, why could she not say no? Did it have to do with the subservient role women were indoctrinated in within the church?

Courting Dad, she went on to say had its challenges. When she had questions and doubts concerning their relationship, he would get insecure and threaten her. He said, "If you don't marry me, I will either kill myself or disappear, and no one will ever know where I am." She was further persuaded to marry him by his sisters who encouraged her, stating their family would be disappointed and heavily impacted if she did not go forward with it. She wondered why?

CHAPTER 3

I have five older brothers and a younger sister. Large families are common, especially as help was needed on the farm. Birth control was not allowed and still is not practiced with the Amish today. The thought was that God put us on the earth to replenish it.

Home deliveries were normal in the country. Mom told me I got stuck in the birth canal, and I wouldn't come out until Dr. Swanson, the country doctor, came and turned me around. When I came out, I was blue, unresponsive to normal stimulus, and not breathing. They dipped me in warm and then cold water until I started breathing. They probably spanked me. I'm grateful! God gave me a good mind because it could have gone a different direction. My cradle was a cardboard box. We were poor.

To this day, my brothers tell me they were very excited to have a sister. My first name was Martha. Dad wanted me named that. But Mom wanted to name me Marianne. Somehow Grandma convinced Dad that he should allow Mom to name me. Three days later, my name became Marianne. He was disgruntled but went along with it. After all, both grandmas were named Mary. In Amish families, names are often repeated.

Sixteen months later, my sister Irma was born. Mom had a few miscarriages in between my older brothers' births. Dad would be very upset with her for losing them. One such event was twins. He was really upset with her over that one. More children was a good sign of his manhood. After Irma, miscarriages became more frequent. She would have more blood loss each time. The doctor wanted her to have a hysterectomy, but Dad was against it. In the end, he realized Mom was not going to successfully carry any more babies to full term, and the loss of so much blood was threatening her life. He reluctantly went along with the doctor, and the hysterectomy was performed.

A few days after the surgery, he had his way with Mom, thinking they had removed all her organs and he would never have sex with her again. A week later, Doctor Swanson came to the house to follow up on Mom. After he checked her, he stormed around the house angrily, swearing under his breath. Dad had disregarded his instructions to not touch her until she healed for a good six weeks. I'm guessing the doctor's explanation to him as to what extent he was removing Mom's organs probably did not happen or make sense to him. Also little did he know that Dad would not wait or have regard for Mom for that length of time. Mom had to submit to his needs. She said the doctor took a walk with Dad for a man-to-man talk. He never divulged to her what they talked about.

CHAPTER 4

At two years old, there was a big change in our family. Dad wanted a car! That would mean leaving the Amish. He found a farm seven miles outside of the Amish community to buy. With forty acres, he could put the boys to work on it while he found a job distributing bottled gas for kitchen stoves in the community. Farming was the main occupation of the Amish, so the more children, the more farm help.

Commonly what happens when one joins the Amish church in their late teens or early twenties occurs after rumspringa. Should one decide to leave after having joined the church with its rules, then excommunication is implemented by the Amish leaders. Leaving is a serious offense, probably the worst one can commit in the church.

After leaving the church, Mom now faced the loss of community, her parents, brothers, and sisters. Excommunicated from the church by the bishops and shunned by all, she is rejected, an outcast, a deceived sinner who strayed from the requirements and given over to Satan. She feared the unknown or the consequences she would no longer be allowed to eat or fellowship with them or be invited to weddings or funerals. If she or Dad were allowed to attend, they would be put on the back row. She cried, begging Dad not to do it, but his mind was made up; and he would not listen to her reason.

The fear of going to hell was very real for Mom. The structure of living life simply separately from the world in modest attire was a core belief for her to go to heaven. Any change moving away from the Amish could lead her to disobedience to be tempted to become like the world. After all, that is why the Amish broke away from the Mennonites years ago. They were becoming too worldly and allowed many things that the world endorsed.

Once that door was opened to change things like buttons on dresses or hooks and eyes on the guy's pants, it was believed to be an open door to do more things that the world endorsed. That would be considered prideful following the lust of the world. That was a command to not be like the world. This is based on Romans 12:2, which says, *"And be not conformed to this world but be ye transformed by the renewing of your mind, that you may prove what is that good and acceptable and perfect will of God."* She was taught that once you have tasted the right way (being Amish) and given yourself to it, to leave is damnable. Your soul would be lost. Outsiders could eat with her Amish family, but she and Dad could not.

For Mom, divorce was not an option as no one in the church divorces. In very rare incidents, I have seen the "wayward" partner leave the church. This is usually the man. The wife does not want to leave, so her "wayward" partner will leave his wife and the church. Mom had seven children. Submission is what a woman does toward her husband *"as unto the Lord,"* as one scripture by Paul in the Bible says. She said she and her father-in-law fought hard about their leaving. In the end, she knew she had to submit. In the Amish church, as well as the Mennonites, submission to your husband was an unquestionable part of life and her salvation. She had to submit even if she did not want to.

One evening, as Mom was looking out the window, as she had done many times before, she asked God to help her make sense of her difficult struggle. In the distance, she saw Christ looking at her, and He said, "You are okay to leave." This gave her peace.

What I know about then

I had seen that sometimes when a woman is required to submit, especially against her will, she looks for ways to gain her power back by manipulating circumstances in the marriage to her advantage. One of these is by not talking, even pouting about her misery.

BEHIND THE SCENE

This silently shames her husband, making him feel insecure. She can then control and manipulate him subconsciously to dominate the relationship.

Or she can be passive and bury her will, which will cause her to be a doormat for people to walk on. By becoming a doormat, I have yet to see a controlling husband who will love and respect his wife. These women often have stories of having suffered childhood abuse, either sexual or verbal. As a result, the wife continues to devalue herself, losing hope that she will ever become who God made her to be, both personally or in the relationship.

Growing up in church, the teaching was that women are the weaker vessel. Physically I believe men are usually built stronger. However, will we always be considered less than, devalued, and flawed emotionally and spiritually? There were times when I had discussions with Mennonite ministers in which there was an underlying implication that women are more easily seduced and emotional. Women opened the door to Satan, persuaded Adam, and destroyed God's image of man. They believe the woman was made for the men to save them from submitting to sin or in the worst case, prostitution. Is that why submission is important? Or does submission have a more meaningful application?

If there is any element of truth in this, then is this not a curse that women are subject to forever because of what Eve did? I pray not! We will bruise the head of the serpent. Genesis 3:15 confirms this: *"And I will put enmity between thee and the woman and between thy seed and her seed; it shall bruise thy head and thou shalt bruise his heel."* I like what Paul says in Romans 16:20, *"And the God of peace shall bruise Satan under your feet shortly."*

I have a spirit, soul, and body as a man does. We are different yet responsible to grow spiritually every day. It is a daily process of becoming a new creature because the old has passed away. Christ wiped away the old law of being a slave to sin. We are *all* made new in Him. This is available for women as well as men. He will never leave us nor forsake us.

I am a mom. I nurture. My brain functions differently than a man's. I need to be loved not only because I do things for the family, but also I need to be cherished, listened to, held in my husband's arms, and told that I'm loved. Spiritual union brings great peace. It is knowing God's love at an intimate heart level. My Heavenly Father loves me regardless of what I am or am not: *"So God created man in His own image, after our likeness"* (Genesis 1:27 KJV). *We* are a reflection of Him, male and female, in His image.

As a woman I embrace who I am. My soul in its aloneness wants a companion. This desire for a connection is not seduction or a lustful expression. It is what our Maker puts inside of us to experience, coming out of our aloneness to become a part of God and the other person. However, attraction is not always linked to love, as it often ends with a seeking to fulfill needs without the fulfillment of love. To honor the other is to highly value, to prize, and to not take lightly, giving the other worth. Honor allows God's heart for the other person to open up, thereby giving them an opportunity for their intimacy with God to be a reality. Is this not the kingdom that Christ talks about?

When Christ came, He was the ultimate sacrifice. He does not love us more or less because of what we do. Has God finished changing us? I don't believe so. Women had no rights especially in the Old Testament. The culture in that time was that they were used as property and traded for material goods as was livestock. Today it is much better, and it is still changing.

God, Christ, and the Holy Spirit are always seeking communion and intimacy. God has many names, some masculine and some feminine. He calls Himself El Shaddai, which means the many-breasted one. The root word for *Elohim* in Hebrew is *feminine*, another name He calls himself. He took Eve out of Adam's side, not his little toe. I believe they are to work side by side, the woman respecting him and the man loving her.

Adam and Eve were put in the garden to care for the earth and to rule over it. Spiritually they were to overcome the dominion Satan had on earth before Adam and Eve got here. We know that did not happen.

God has always wanted a relationship with Him. When Moses went up the mountain to meet with God in the wilderness, God originally wanted to meet with the people, but they said, "No, Moses, you go." He gave the Ten Commandments as a marriage covenant to them. What I am trying to say here is that He is looking for His bride to be alongside Himself, male and female. He is coming back for His Bride.

God knew all this would happen. Why? Because Christ was crucified before the foundation of the earth. I don't know all the answers, but I do believe that God has gifted men to lead. They take responsibility for their household. It's a gift that reminds me of the kind shepherd that loves and cares for his family, helping His children to come to know God.

CHAPTER 5

Back to my story. From Amish to Mennonite, Dad bought an old car. It was all we could afford. We were no longer riding in a buggy drawn by a horse. For the first time, we were allowed to take pictures of each other, which was considered idolatrous before. We could hang pictures on the wall. The Mennonite white head covering was smaller, showing more hair. Buttons were allowed instead of pins. I still felt that we as women were more restricted than were the men. The men could wear regular pants with zippers instead of hooks and eyes. Our John Deere tractor got rubber tires instead of metal spokes.

Many things were similar. Our wearing of the cape, covering our front bodice, was required at church on Sundays to minimize our curvatures. Our dress lengths were a little shorter but were still below the knees. And no splashy floral prints. All this was to stay modest so as not to tempt or draw attention from the men or tempt them. Our hair had to be parted in the middle. Men were not allowed to wear neckties. Radios and worldly music were forbidden.

We did not fit in well. Looking back, I am sure we looked like Amish people driving a car. Dad did shave off his beard. The young people had their opinions of what was fashionable within the Mennonite church. In our transition from Amish to Mennonites, our Amish clothes did not fit in within their norm. I always felt as if our whole family did not fit in. Our clunker of a car would pull up after church to pick up Mom, my sister, and I at the church door. The snickers and comments were heard with disdain as the young people made fun of our clothes, our car, and my brothers. This was very painful and humiliating for me and my sister. Inside we were alone with no value.

My two oldest brothers married in the Mennonite church. They had a few cousins as friends who had also left the Amish church near the same time we did. Their friendships last to this day. My other siblings endured shame and loss of respect, never daring to speak out against their mockery They left, being disillusioned and found wives outside the church.

Within the Mennonite church, there were cliques. It felt like families leading the church were well dressed and had an attitude of superiority. They presented themselves with an air of being all put together in a neat package. Looking back, I wonder if my own insecurity made me more sensitive to this. Later I saw it as a false humility mixed with pride in their attitude of being right. Another clique was made up of the more common people with which we also did not fit. The fresh stench of us coming out of the Amish church was not something they could embrace. We were shy, backward, and unassuming. We felt rejected and pushed away, hoping and trying to fit in. It didn't work. We did not belong, especially with the young people. I promised myself that they would not do that to me when I grew up. After all, I was going to be a missionary and a nurse. I'd show them.

At that time, it seemed there was no way for any approval or acceptance from people in the church. Their air of specialness exuded itself. Today as I look back, I also understand another aspect of it. I have mentored young underprivileged teens. They look at my house and car. I see the wheels turning in their brain. They think I have no clue as to their difficulties in life or lack of money. It is a challenge for them to tell me of their struggles because they think I could not relate to their misfortunes. I assure them it was not always so. When I was a child, I am sure that I viewed the leadership in the church in a similar way.

My takeaway today is this: one never knows what people go through. Everyone has a story, one with hardship and controversy in it. Today I am blessed. I have learned to love first, giving and honoring people, even those who are not capable of returning it. The difficulties in my life have given me compassion for others that are hurting from abuse. My example is Christ.

Back to my story

Our house at our new location on the farm was small and primitive. Two bedrooms upstairs was where my five brothers slept, and downstairs there was one bedroom, which my sister and I shared with Mom and Dad. Our "outhouse" fifty feet from the house was just that—an outside two seated toilet with catalogs for wiping. In the winter when it was too cold to go outside to the outhouse, we had pots to use that were emptied daily. They were our vessels of dishonor.

I was probably six or seven years old when the kitchen addition was put onto the living room. My parents moved their bedroom to what was the living room. Irma and I were glad to get our own room, but that did not negate hearing the interaction between Mom and Dad in bed at night. The walls were thin, and Mom's complaints were loud enough for us to hear. She was not happy.

We got electricity as well. I loved flipping the switch and watching the lights go on and off. No more smelly lanterns in the house and struggling to see after dark. Or reading around the table or taking the lantern from room to room to find what we were looking for. A sink to the side of the countertop of our new kitchen had a small hand pump that brought in water from the well outside. We no longer had to fetch water from the well outside to bring into the house.

Dad's old car got a new look. Mom didn't like the old faded color on it, so she picked up her paint and brush and painted it burgundy. There were a few brush streaks, but it was an improvement I thought, but it depended on whose opinion you asked. The first time Mom tried to drive, she turned when Dad told her to and drove it straight off the gravel road into the ditch! Standing at a distance in the neighbor's yard, I cried as I watched it nearly capsize. My older brothers laughed.

BEHIND THE SCENE

Baths were not frequent. Mom would heat up water on the woodstove and pour it in an oversized tub on the porch. Irma and I would have baths first, then my brothers would follow using the same water adding to it as they bathed. Mom made a makeshift shower. She would take a bucket with a hole in it and hang it above her head on the porch and wash under the small stream after dark. I don't ever recall Dad taking a bath or shower. He may have if Mom fussed at him often enough. The Amish are not known to shower often or do they use deodorant. Mom was weighed down with life, and headaches were a common occurrence, putting her in bed for days.

CHAPTER 6

School started for me when I was six years old. Dad would not let me go sooner. Too much knowledge was of the devil. And I had to learn English from my family first. Pennsylvania Dutch was my first language.

One afternoon, walking home from school, the nearly two miles seemed to take forever. Most of my brothers were walking ahead of my sister and me as they usually did. The air was unsettled. The summer heat was hot and humid. My sister and I kicked up the dirt under our feet, creating a cloud of dust as we "putzed" along.

I thought to myself. I liked our little one room schoolhouse where all the grades were taught. Each grade was brought to the front of the room when it was their turn to have the teacher's attention. I loved listening to the other class discussions. Recess was a time of baseball and making stick forts. Sometimes when we misbehaved, our teacher would draw a circle on the blackboard, and we would have to put our nose in it. That was a ring of humiliation. We were almost home trudging up the last big hill. It seemed like such a long walk. Car rides were for rainy or snowy days only.

Back to my inner world

The stress of life was wearing away at Mom's will to live. She stayed in bed for what seemed like weeks. No one would talk about it. She would not cook, help us, or participate in any of the family events. She was absent for evening meals and lunch preparation for school. The family doctor came by to visit. The adults, including the doctor, Dad and my oldest brother, spoke in muffled tones. There was a sadness in the air. Dad was quiet, angry, and sullen.

Why did Mom and Dad not love each other? Maybe they did in the only way they were shown by their parents, with no outward emotion or expression. They never hugged each other. Nor was there any encouragement or appreciation for the other person expressed. Was there any emotion in it? Was the only closeness, physical sex, in bed at night after dark, which did not sound good?

I don't recall ever being given a hug or told that I was loved or appreciated. After all, that could make me very prideful, which was something to be feared. Nor did they mention that my siblings and I ever did a good job. Work was expected. Today I wonder, as I see the self-hatred and self-rejection that my brothers carry, that if encouragement and praise for a good job would have been better? If only we had been taught confidence and self-satisfaction in a job well done instead of fearing wrongful pride.

I recall one day walking home from school, my "English" neighbor stopped his car and asked, "Honey, would you like to come over to play with Jane today after school?" That shook me up. No one had ever called me honey. I blushed. He had called his daughter that on other occasions as I recall. I learned at their home, they called each other honey. I had never heard those terms of endearment.

The road past our house provided some interesting discoveries for us. There were various shapes and sizes of rocks along the road. Mom would groan as I dragged some of them home. I would break them open with a hammer to see what colors were in them. Once I found a fossil of clam shells and a tiny fish. Wow! Does that mean where we lived was once underwater?

In the Midwest, the rain would make the dirt into a thick, sticky flour paste. One could sink into the mud six inches. Our car would get stuck on more than one occasion. Then it was push time, and we would push, trying not to get behind the rear wheels to get splattered with mud. In the winter, we would slip into the ditch much too often. Then only the tractor could pull us out. The road became impassable. We would park our car on the gravel road that was down the hill from our house and walk up the hill. Our neighbor was not happy about us walking across his field, especially if we stepped on his crops.

We were almost home trudging up the last big hill. It seemed like such a long walk. Car rides were for rainy or snowy days only. Continuing on our walk home that day, my mind kept wandering. What would it be like to be English like my classmates? What would it be like to wear pretty dresses and to cut and put curls in my hair? Or to wear pedal pushers? I interrupted my thoughts abruptly, remembering the Bible teaches us not to dress like a man. No pants allowed. After all, we were taught and believed we knew the right ways to get to heaven. It's wrong to draw attention to ourselves by the outward show of beauty. I am to be beautiful on the inside and not to adorn myself or braid my hair as the woman is talked about in Proverbs. To be "English" was to dress like the world, and the world was a "bad place." However, if I were God, making me a girl would not have been my choice.

Life was filled with chores on the farm and seemed like such a *druvel* (a Pennsylvania Dutch expression meaning "a big bother"). Mom would beg the boys to go milk the cows. In the mornings, sometimes she would have to go milk them herself, and in the evening, the boys would ignore her and continue doing whatever they were doing. They were getting too big to spank. I hated the discord that resulted when Mom wanted them to do what they were not willing to do. Not only did I want the conflict to stop, but I learned that if I did what was asked, the conflict stopped. So at the age of seven, I went to get the cows from the field and start milking them.

"Come on, hurry up," my brothers called again. Why did I always have to do what they wanted? We got to the top of the hill, and I could see home. I was shocked to see there was an ambulance parked in the yard by the front door. My heart was pounding with fear in my chest. What was wrong with Mom? She had been so sad. She lay in bed for what seemed like days. We were left to do things for ourselves.

The adults were speaking in muffled tones so Irma and I could not understand. As we walked into the bedroom where the voices were coming from, the strong paramedics were lifting Mom from her bed to the gurney. She looked at us with sad and loving eyes as she told us she hoped to be back. Many years later, I was told the family doctor thought it was a heart attack, but it turned out to be a nervous breakdown.

With Mom in the hospital, the main responsibility of the evening meal and cleanup was mostly Irma's and my responsibility. My older brother, who I will call Mose, did help with meals; they were simple. One of my favorites was milk with broken-up bread, sugar, and bananas called *brokul* soup. Another one was upside-down pot pie. Fruit in the bottom of the pan and a batter on top to bake. It was so good with milk. Then there was *rivel* soup. We used eggs from our chickens and flour smushed together until "just larger than crumb" and added in hot milk and stirred until creamy.

One evening, he confided to me that it was he who had called the doctor and the paramedics because he was afraid Mom was going to die. Dad was very angry with him because it would cost too much money for the doctor and hospital. I knew in my heart that if Mom was gone too long and Dad did not get his sexual appetite met, that life would be miserable for him and us. Only many years later did I remember what really happened to me at that time.

Things were getting pretty upside down and frightening with Mom not being home. One day, some ladies from the church came to clean and do laundry. They brought a box of shoes of various sizes for my sister and me. When we outgrew our current shoes, we would go find another pair in a box under the bed. Shoe stores did not get our business. I don't ever recall shoe shopping at a store until I got older.

Clothes were piled up, it seemed like everywhere. The church ladies went through every closet and organized, cleaning and washing everything. It felt invasive and embarrassing. I recall being horrified at the screams coming from the closet as they found a nest of mice. I also knew that the mess and the mice would come up at the next quilting at the church because that is where they discussed such matters. I was privy to many of those gossiping conversations about people and their affairs. The pastor and his wife were also subject material. It was addicting, but I knew that it was wrong. Sometimes I think it makes people feel important because they know more than others. It makes them feel good even though it is none of anyone's business.

Back to the mice. If only they knew what the rats looked like around the "slop bucket" at the top of the basement stairs, they would really scream. We would put scraps of food in this bucket and then feed it to the pigs. They would eat anything disgusting. Occasionally some scraps would drop outside the bucket. That is when a few rats would look at me as I opened the door to put more scraps in. Their glowing demonic eyes would look at me in surprise. I slammed the door shut, screaming!

Now concerning mice, that was different if we found one in the house. The air would fill with screams and excitement as we grabbed brooms and sticks. Doors slammed shut. Furniture was moved quickly as we turned things upside down until the critter was found. It darted across the floor, dodging attacking brooms until it was finally knocked silly, leading to its demise, and then disposed of.

Dad was getting more withdrawn and sullen, muttering things about Mom but mostly saying nothing. It had been a month. News was scarce. Dad would make the twenty-five-mile trek once a week to visit her and return saying nothing of when she was coming home or how she was doing.

One Saturday it happened. We were all so excited. Mom came home! She looked very tired but was so happy to see us. She had spent two weeks in the hospital and two weeks at the head Mennonite pastor's home. There she was encouraged and counseled, which allowed her to rest and gain her strength. She had experienced a nervous breakdown. Dad was visibly angry, complaining that she was doing it all to get attention.

I learned early that it was more important to help others and care for them before considering myself. Neglect or disregard for myself was what made others accomplish what they needed. After all, Mom did that. Work was part of feeling good about myself. I bolstered my sense of self-worth by all the things I got accomplished. I watched Mom struggle with the weight of her daily workload. I wanted to help eliminate that load for her, but the chores and work were always there staring at us. At the end of the day, deep down inside, I was missing something.

Eventually, I became a caretaker for my mom and felt the responsibility for the family. It made me a nurturer, a fixer, and a mom to my mom. This carried over to my adult life. I was rewarded by appreciation for doing. It was my salvation. Working hard gave me satisfaction, but it did not make me love who I was.

Concern for others rather than focusing on myself was a cover-up for me. I did not have to look at my own stuff. To help them as selfless as this seemed, it put me under a heavy burden, which was not always mine but theirs to learn to mature in. Their needs would become excessive and oppressive. With difficulty, I learned that it is important for me to be able to say no, especially when I was not doing them a favor. It was important for the individual to learn to carry their own load. It is important that I heal and pull in my boundaries by putting them in place and not losing me in the middle of caring.

There was no appreciation shown from Dad for any of us. Those words were not openly expressed. Nor were words of encouragement expressed. Only instructions and corrections and what is expected of us. We knew that was our role in life. We were expected to do what was right, with no complaining. "It just needs to get done," Mom and Dad would say. "Why haven't you done it?" I hated myself, yet I had to find another way to live. Why did God put me in this family?

Many times, Mom would cope by feeling sorry for herself. Now I understand why. She was criticized for having an opinion. She had all kinds of reasons for feeling as she did, but it didn't help her. She still had to look at her situation and survive. She was trapped with no way out, so it took her into depression, something that was passed down from her mom. She then passed it on to my siblings and their offspring. At the odds of me falling into the same trap as I got older, I knew I needed to find a way to avoid walking in those same footsteps. There had to be other options. I would find them. I kept searching.

Today I don't push depression aside. I question why I have feelings of depression. Is it the anniversary of something traumatic that happened to me? Is it what someone said? Have I been around someone who talked to me about their sad event, and I took that on? Or is it that I have not spent time with God to build up who He is in me? I know He is as close as the air I breathe.

*****

Life on the farm had its good memories. One day a visitor came by. That was a rare event. He was selling a newspaper called *Capper's Weekly*. Mom had no money. She offered him a chicken for payment. He took it, giving her a year's subscription and wrote up the story about the transaction in the newspaper. A chicken for a subscription!

Good childhood memories were making bread, rolls, and doughnuts. Yeast miraculously raised the dough only to be patted down aggressively and put in a baking dish. Doughnuts and cinnamon rolls were made occasionally. We would eat as many as Mom would allow when they came out of the pan of splattering grease. We would put sugar on them, eating them before they cooled off.

When I was ten years old, I took on the household chores such as cleaning, picking up everyone's clothes, and putting things away. They always landed where they took them off, on the floor. Cleaning up the living room felt great. I loved the organization with no clutter. I then moved on to clean the bedrooms and kitchen. My brothers would complain bitterly that I had hid their clothes when they could not find them. Mom occasionally joined in. It was confusing, but I liked it being clean, so I had to decide whether to take the verbal assault from my family or live in chaos.

In the spring, we would help with planting the garden after it was plowed. Mom would pride herself in making straight rows. She would take two poles and tie a string on each one and place one at each end of the row. This was to ensure that the rows were straight. We would be given seeds from a packet and instructed how many we could plant and how far apart the seeds needed to be. Every seed was planted at a different depth. We would help put the dirt over the seeds and pat the dirt down lightly. Watching the little seedlings come up a few weeks later was rewarding. Next we would have to help weed the garden. UGH!

However, it was rewarding to see as I saw the weeds clear out and the veggies have space to grow. Sometimes my hoe would miss and slice my toes. When the harvest came in, vegetables and fruit trees produced, it was then canning time. Stem the strawberries, snap the beans, pick the fruit, and husk the corn. Mom's goal for our size family was one hundred quarts of each food to last us until the next year.

Sometimes we grew hay in the fields. The baler went through the fields, binding up the hay into bales. Using our little tractor, we pulled a gate along the ground, dragging it with a chain to pick up the bales, stacking them on the gate. I was the one who drove the tractor. I learned to drive it before I drove the car. The next step was to get the bales into the second story of the barn. There was a large opening on the side just for this purpose. There were long ropes to carry the load, with a pulley and large curved iron forks that we would stick into the bales. Our tractor then pulled the ropes, lifting them to the rail on the second story. As the bales fell, my brothers would stack them. When it was all done, we would take a rope and make a swing that hung from the metal rail attached to the roof and swing from one side of the barn to the other.

One year, the Heinz corporation contacted us and asked to lease our land to grow tomatoes. That seemed like a good thing as we could make money, and they would bring in outside workers to take care of the crop. On one or two occasions, we had tomato fights in the field of which Mom hosed us down and said, "No more." I'm not sure why, but that lasted for one year. I don't think Mom was fond of the strange people who would come to work in the fields.

Irma was on a different path. She neither share my love for order nor did she think chores and work are related to feeling good about herself. We got along like sisters with an occasional squabble. One of my fond memories of her was going to fetch the cows in the evening to bring them to the barn for milking. On occasion, we would accidentally step on a warm cow patty. We would scream when the mire of poo would ooze up between our toes when we were not watching where we stepped. We were quick to rinse our feet in the creek. We would soon get distracted fetching squiggly tadpoles from the stream and putting them in a bucket. In a few days, it was so disappointing to see them die as we were hoping to see them turn into frogs. Mom said that out of their natural environment, they would die.

Our six cows each had different names. My favorite was Betsy, a brown-and-white Guernsey. She was gentle and an easy one to learn to milk. Some of the others would quickly kick if I hurt them by squeezing their teats to get the milk out. I'd get the milking started, and my brothers would come finish. They could get more milk out of the cows than I could. I squirted my cats sometimes with a stream of milk, aiming at their mouths a few feet away. I usually ended up spraying their faces as they sat on their hind legs waiting with anticipation. As I got older and more experienced, I was able to balance on the T-shaped stool and make foam in the bucket of milk as the streams of milk were more forceful. My brothers, Ben and Rueben, would sometimes sit on the cows and pretend they were riding them. Irma and I followed suit, pretending they were our horses. When Mom found out, she put a stop to it. She said, "Their backs are not strong enough to support you."

I learned what a pitchfork was. We used it to pick up the cow manure mixed with straw to throw it out of the open barn window. This was certainly not what my brothers were interested in doing. If this was not done routinely, the milking area would become ankle-deep in cow manure. With my growing love for order, I would dig those prongs of the pitchfork deep into the mixture of straw and cow manure, then swing it high, hoping to hit the open window. Sometimes my brothers laughed at me because I could not throw the pitchfork high enough and the wall got the carnage.

Gathering the eggs was a simpler task I enjoyed. We had to be reminded to close the door every night to keep out the pesky raccoons that would love to come in and steal the chickens in the middle of the night.

Our dog Muddy was a special gift. She would chase those critters up a tree in the middle of the night, then trek back to our bedroom window and bark to wake us up. This barking ruckus continued until we got up to see what was going on. Dad had to be skillful in getting a good aim with the gun to kill the culprit or it could get away, although Muddy would fight with it. A wounded animal seems a lot more vicious, and we feared for Muddy's life on more than one occasion. One animal she learned not to mess with were the skunks. She would come home and be rubbing her eyes and smell awful.

One morning, Eli, our neighbor across the road, knocked on the door. He was carrying a newborn baby lamb. The mother died during its birth, and the lamb also was nearly dead. He told Mom he didn't think it would live. Mom cleaned it up. Twenty-four hours a day she watched over it, putting it on a feeding schedule with a bottle of warm milk. We would take turns giving it a bottle. It became stronger. We became its parents as it would follow us everywhere. It jumped up on all four legs with delight as only lambs can do.

Eli gave us a second near-death lamb the following year, and Mom again nurtured it around the clock. When they got a little bigger, Dad would take a hatchet and chop off its tail. A very sad day came when Dad was insistent that we have to sell them. I asked Mom who would buy them, and she predicted that they would be butchered. We always needed the money.

Eli, our neighbor, would hire my brothers occasionally to work for him. One summer, Mom instructed me to take a message to the boys in the field across the road: lunch was ready. I climbed the gate (I was proud of my skill) that fenced in a huge flock of turkeys. I was not afraid. Surprisingly they swarmed around me, pecking at me. My height was the same as their heads. My arms hitting at them did nothing. They came at me from all sides. The next thing I knew I was on the ground, swinging and kicking at them. I was convinced they were going to peck me to death. Gratefully, one of my brothers came to my rescue. No one spoke about this scary incident, which to me felt like a near-death experience. It was just life on the farm, and these things happen; therefore, don't overreact.

Some of our other neighbors would bring their farm equipment to take corn from the fields at harvesttime to put into the storage bin. Their payment was a certain portion of the corn. As the machine shelled the corn, the grain was piped into a separate bin. We would get up on the rafters and jump into the corn. That was a very scary jump of approximately twelve-to-fifteen feet but so exhilarating.

*****

Our house caught on fire. When my brothers took off their pants at night, they dropped them next to the warm stovepipe that went through their room. The pipe went from the wooden stove in the living room downstairs through the bedrooms upstairs and out the roof. It warmed the upstairs as well as downstairs. Thankfully, Mom smelled the smoke early, woke up the boys, and it was soon put out. The floor around the pipe had some black charred areas.

The wash house, where we did our wash, was twenty feet from the house. We had a large cast-iron pot set on a sturdy metal frame. There was an area to build a fire in that framework to be able to heat things in the large pot. It could hold many gallons of liquid. We would make laundry soap by mixing lye and grease. When it melted, we would mix it by stirring it. We would allow it to cool, then cut it into chunks and use it for laundry soap. Or there were days when the Mennonite women would get-together to make vegetable soup for canning. Each would bring a different vegetable from their garden to add to the mix. They would clean what seemed like an enormous number of jars to can the soup for the winter months. The best was when someone would bring meat to add to the soup. Along with the vegetables came children, and we had fun playing.

On one such occasion of making soap, my brother, who I will call Ben, built a fire. He carelessly left a trail of wood kindling outside the opening to the fire. With time, the fire spread, making its way outside the opening to the walls of the wash house. By this time, it was dark outside. Mom and Dad were gone to do chores for the neighbors. Ben, Rueben, Irma, and I were home alone. We kept hearing crackles. When we looked outside, the large wash house was fully engulfed in flames. I immediately lifted the receiver of the old party line phone hanging on the wall and called my neighbors to tell them I needed the fire whistle. They did not understand, so I realized I needed to call the operator for the fire whistle. She understood and dispatched the fire department. (When we heard sirens, we always referred to it as the fire whistle). My brothers took buckets of water to throw on the fire, but it was too hot to get close.

The volunteer fire department could not get to our house because it had rained, and the road past our house was impassible. They carried tanks and hoses up the hill through our neighbors' field and put water on the house due to the extreme heat. They were afraid it was going to catch fire. Mom and Dad coming home from helping a neighbor saw the flames from a distance and thought the house was on fire. Mom was panicking, wondering if her children were safe. With every laborious step, her feet would sink into the deep mud, walking up the hill alongside the volunteer firefighters who were coming in from neighboring communities carrying their tanks. When she got to the top of the hill, she saw with great relief the four of us standing on the front lawn. The fire department put us there away from the house and the fire to make sure we were safe.

Our pet animals were outdoor animals. I'd keep trying to sneak my kittens or puppies inside the house to play, but Mom would make me take them outside. I loved the little yellow baby ducks. They would line up behind Irma and me and follow us like we were their mothers. Our dog Muddy had many litters of puppies each year. Irma and I would dress the baby puppies in doll clothes and pretend we were in church. Once in a while, we would have to take them out and threaten to spank them if they were too "rowdy" in church. We played that many times. That was our favorite make-believe playtime.

Christmas at our house was not celebrated. My parents had very little money, and gifts were not exchanged. Nor was it celebrated in the church with gift giving or decorations such as a tree or lights, so I would collect pine branches and put my own decorations on them. The church did teach it was Christ's birthday.

One Christmas, Mom put away enough money to get Irma and me "English" dolls that opened and closed their eyes. Prior to that, we must have had a dozen rag dolls to play with. There was not enough money to go around to get my brothers anything. They were angry, as they should have been, and gave Mom a tough time for showing favor to us. I think Mom, to her surprise, learned that what she did in preferring Irma and me was not a good thing. They teased us for being "the favored ones."

There was all kinds of work to be done with such a large family. Monday was laundry day. A fire was made under the large outdoor metal kettle, and buckets of hot water would be transferred into the washing machine, which was moved to the basement. This was difficult in the wintertime. The clothesline outside carried all nine loads of laundry. It was an all-day event. One time I got my fingers too close to the wringer as I was feeding the clothes through it. I watched as the roller began squeezing, then swallowing up first my fingers, then my hand, and then up my arm. I was unable to flip the switch off. Mom ran to my rescue to trip the roller. I wondered if it would have flattened my whole body or tried to tear my arm off!

When the clothes dried, Mom would bury her face in them, smelling the fresh laundry scent. "They smell so good," she would exclaim. On cold winter days, we would hang the clothes inside the house on ropes that were strung from doorframe to doorframe held in place by a nail. Irma and I could play hide-and-seek in the rows of clothes in the living room. That was a fun maze, but Mom put a stop to that.

On Tuesdays we would iron and continue to put clothes away. Before we got electricity, Mom would cook on an antique wood-burning stove. It had many uses as its warmth heated the kitchen. On the flat top, the heavy iron was placed on the stove top to heat up. (This was a tradition left over from when we were Amish when we had no electricity). She had to time it right because it could burn the clothes if it got too hot.

Hankies and pillowcases were my first ironing challenge. I would take it over to the ironing board and use it until it got cold, then put it back on the stove to reheat as Mom instructed. Sometimes my fingers got too close to the iron, leaving burn marks. It was all a part of the package we were given to make life work. Sometimes Mom would put Mercurochrome on it. It was an orange substance that burned, and yes, the disinfectant part of it was mercury.

BEHIND THE SCENE

Sewing was much more interesting to me. Mom would sew all our clothes, including shirts and pants for the men in the family. We also made our own curtains for windows and quilts for the beds—beautiful quilts that we as Amish and Mennonites are still known for today. When I turned seven years of age, Mom would show me how to sew simple things on her "treadle" sewing machine. I would study how to make doll clothes and sew them, making many mistakes. Quilt blocks came later, which required sewing in straight lines. I loved it. Except when the edges of the blocks did not line up, I would have to tear out the seams and resew. Mom was particular.

After she finished the quilt top, mixing all the varied beautiful colors, she would put a backing on it and invite people in for a quilting day. She enjoyed being with other women. They talked a lot. She insisted that I learn to do the stitching on the quilt. If the stitches were too big or uneven, she would have me rip them out. The needle had to include the bottom layer of material. I would sit and admire the beautiful, even stitches that the women around the quilt were sewing with their needles and thread. Irma hated to do that stuff. She would look for opportunities to play.

Later, Mom showed me the basics of making a simple dress with a pattern or how to make a pattern from a dress. That was my favorite. Even though I made many mistakes, I learned from them. Maybe that is where I learned it was good to tear things apart and start over again in life.

One time we went to our grandpa's house for a quilting for a friend. Mom loved getting together with her friends. My attention span for quilting didn't last long, so my sister and I went off to play with the other kids. We went upstairs to one of the bedrooms. Because they were Amish, there was a large box of matches hanging on the wall that they used to light their lanterns. It caught my attention. I showed the girls how to light the matches by striking them on the side of the box. We would watch the match burn for a bit, blow it out, and throw it under the bed to hide the evidence. This went on until most of the box had been lit. One of the girls told their mom. I had already moved on to another adventure outside when my mom confronted me. She said that I was the initiator of the mischief. I was so ashamed that I denied it. It bothered me as I thought of myself as a truth teller. Why did I deny it? Lying was not something I did. However, to cover up a shameful secret, that was something I could do. Even later in my life, many dark secrets had to remain so. They had no name, and they had to go away as if it was nothing.

My kittens were an important part of my world. Rarely would Mom allow Irma and me to sleep with them. We would dress them in doll clothes and wrap them in blankets. As they got older, they started coughing and wheezing. Mom said our farm had a lung disease that gave them this lethal cough. They would eventually die. One day I watched Dad take my favorite sick, thin, and dying cat, and put her into a paper bag. He threw her in his truck and drove off to work. I begged him to tell me what he did with her. Finally, Mom said he threw her over the bridge into the river. I was heartbroken as I wondered what the cat went through during the last moments of its life. With sadness, I still remember this well.

CHAPTER 7

One of my favorite things to do was to climb trees and stay there to get away from things. It was safe. I still wished I was a boy. They didn't seem to have to work so hard. I had to submit to my brothers' wishes when by a simple nod of the head, I was expected to follow them wherever they chose to take advantage of me. A memory at three years old was as I was looking down toward my feet, I saw one of my brothers putting objects in my private parts. I didn't understand why. I do not recall what happened after that or his first sexual advancement toward me to have intercourse. I would think it would have been very painful. It is a memory that is still hidden away. I was so trapped and alone in my inside world where I would not dare talk about it. It was my prison with no way out.

Being Amish is not who I am today, but my story is. I write to you, my brothers and sisters, who follow the traditions of the church and its rules of what we "should do" that is followed. God loves you as much as He loves me. He does not want you to have to put up a front or smother your secrets. He wants you to be free from what is hidden, whether you remain Amish or Mennonite or other. The secrets that too many children have had to bear, I now know are more common than what I thought when I was growing up. "It has to be just my family," I thought. I am writing this because people are too ashamed to bring this to the forefront, not knowing what to do with it. There has to be a safe way to talk about it without telling the whole world, allowing families and children to heal.

What I know now about then

Sexual abuse in childhood steals one's innocence and exposes them to the adult world, which they are not capable of handling. They do not know what to do with it mentally, emotionally, and psychologically. Sexual abuse will absolutely destroy one's true being by fundamentally erasing any sense of worth, believing they are trash, useless, and feeling used. So one of the ways to survive is to bury it deep. This becomes an open door for Satan to attach his tentacles to the dark secrets of shame, isolation, and self-hate. It can even open the door for the survivor to have a sexual appetite (by exposure to the adult world), all the while hating it when it happens. Then there is guilt and shame when it is enjoyed or pleasurable. Sometimes the perpetrator says, "You know you like this," shaming them as if it was their fault.

I did not know how to express my emotions. When I was in kindergarten after school one day, I started to cry and I couldn't stop; I had no idea why. The teacher took me home. Mom ignored me after my inability to express to her why I was crying. The next day the same thing happened. Everyone ignored me; crying was not a good thing. Stuffing my emotions, blocking them away from the surface of my interactions with people worked for me.

I would wonder for years when the ministers would say, "Your true nature is evil," I knew I was flawed because of the sexual sin. I began to question, "What is the truth of my being?" Is it what I had feared deep down at my core? I was never good enough. Could the black stain on my soul ever be removed? I had to put up a front because if anyone knew who I was on the inside, they would walk away and abandon me. I had to find a way to become perfect in what others expected of me. The last thing I wanted was to be judged as a bad person. If I strove to follow the rules to become disciplined, then it would cover my shame in the hopes of making it go away. All of this I have learned is "sin" consciousness and not "God" consciousness.

Why was I subjected to such sexual slavery by my older brothers? I neither know the words nor did I know how to explain it to my mom. How could I? Sex was a dirty secret. Our life of poverty, clouded with shame, separate from the world in dress and action further isolated me. My secrets did not allow me to discuss this with anyone. Somehow it was my fault, I reasoned. I must have done something very wrong to cause this to happen. Sometimes I wondered what it would be like to be loved for just being me.

Later in life, I learned that the rules of the church put on me a greater "I can't" rather than "I can." The I "cannot" made me defensive in most areas of my life. I felt the need to defend myself constantly. Was my whole life a defense? Why? When outsiders saw me, they would ask why I dressed the way I did. I would defend it but never felt like I was able to convince them to join in following my God. Is that why evangelism in the community was not productive?

The world judges by outside appearance. What could I change for them to see my love for Christ first rather than my appearance? My thinking was that if my focus was on what I wore like the covering on my head, then that would reflect who I was. Would that get to their curiosity? Was that my lead-in for them to ask about the Christ who was the center of my being? How could I get them to see Christ first? What I discovered was, it is more important to allow Christ to be what attracts people to the character of who He is in me.

When people see me today, I want them to see who God is in me rather than be drawn to my dress first. Personally, I believe one can dress in such a way. My dress is a reflection of who I am. God made me in His image, wonderfully and worthy of being loved. He said after He created man that it is good. That means I am good. He does not make junk. If I do not know there is anything good in me, then I will strive to be disciplined on the outside and on the inside; I will never measure up. It is not about the dress standards of the church that gives me salvation. If it were, I would always fall short.

Dressing modestly in society is important. I believe there are norms to dress in what is attractive and not provocative. God wants us to be beautiful. Bold colors are healing for me. Look at the flowers, the butterflies, the rainbow, and the colors in the sunrise or sunset. He dresses them so beautifully. Even the beautiful colors in quilts that the Amish put together are done so well.

I wonder if that is why Satan hates us so much because when he sees us, he is reminded of what he lost. He lost as the illuminated one which reflected God's light back to God. Today we are the reflection of Christ's light and love back to God. Salvation makes us beautiful!

More important than my focus on outward appearance is to ask for God's fruit of His Spirit. Love, kindness, longsuffering, gentleness, joy, and peace are a few of those. I am not there yet, but I am constantly growing as I ask for more of these fruits. This is my hunger to be like my Heavenly Pappa.

CHAPTER 8

A few years ago, I had an unusual experience. It was in the early morning hours when it seemed like I was half awake. Where was I? Was it a dream? Or was it a vision? There was darkness all around me. I was disoriented as I reached out to touch the dark, the walls felt soft around me. Trying to orient myself, I knew I was not in the woods in the middle of the night. I then saw my knees pulled up to my chest, head down, and my arms free. My chest burned, and my stomach was upset. In the distance, I saw a round ball of orange-red light. The most disturbing part was what I was feeling. It was utter hopelessness and self-abhorrence. I was sad and alone, not feeling wanted by Mom or Dad. Can someone please blow out the flame to my life? I did not want to live or be born. Was I still in the womb? Was it a memory? Why, God, did you create me?

In my early childhood and teenage years, and now as I think about it, my whole life I have asked questions, searching for answers as to "why." My fight was to make some kind of sense of my life. Much of my childhood I blanked out trying not to remember it. I believed it was not important to go back to relive it. The benefits of pushing it aside outweighed the pain of rehashing it.

I needed relationships with people who would accept me and allow me to be close when I wanted to be close or to be alone when I needed to without rejection. I needed to be alone more often. That did not happen. I ached for it. I can remember feeling that I would do anything in the world to have the kind of friend, like a loving dad, who would just put their arms around me and hold me, caring for me without having to give anything back. God's promise to me is, in God's kingdom, a child gets their needs met. They don't inherit anything from God because of their performance but because of their place as a much-loved child.

As adults, people sometimes become the image of that which they hate. Or there are times they project onto others what is wrong with themselves. Other times when we think about something a great deal, it can become our reality. When people hurt us, they speak words that we believe to be true. The abusers make statements like, "You know you wanted this." Many children grow up to spend their entire lives believing it was their fault that they were molested. That information, at the moment of strong emotion, becomes a heart trauma and belief. At the time of this painful emotion, it becomes the critical judge of their lives.

Words mark and define what children think about themselves. Especially if words are taken from the Bible to correct a child by putting guilt, telling them that they are bad when being punished. This burns shame into that child's soul that they are bad. How one sees the Heavenly Father is based on how one's earthly father was. If a dad is quiet and does not interact, the child sees God as distant, absent, and unresponsive when talked to. Wouldn't it be better to discuss with them what they did and what they could have done differently? Of course, there are consequences for bad decisions. We are all flawed; however, love rules as you enable the child to self-correct by encouraging them.

Abuse obliterates any self-worth. It isolates and shames the very core of one's being. It can be verbal or physical. I would do good things to give myself worth. I learned to please. I learned to blend into any situation, hating confrontation. I became a people pleaser, always helping. Hard work is very important in the Amish and Mennonite culture. My dad would often say, *"That if any would not work, neither should he eat!"* (2 Thessalonians 3:10 KJV). Work became a big part of my salvation. When I did things to please, I felt good about myself. The people around me felt good about me, too, silently affirming my worth.

BEHIND THE SCENE

Looking at my life, I can see where "submission" as taught by the Mennonites and Amish started impacting my life at a young age. I gave in to this type of obedience by not caring about my wishes but to care more for others. As an adult, I learned that this is control. Although it had different faces, my reactions were the same. I had no voice; no utterance would come out of my mouth as I went along with the desires of my brothers who took control. This is where it started for me. Later in life, this pattern continued in unhealthy ways by giving in to church leadership first, then a spouse. In unhealthy control, the controller demands that things be done without consideration or input from anyone else. I now know the controller can be a man or woman. Just because you are a man and your place is to be the spiritual head, this does not make you a godly spiritual authority. Christ gave Himself for the church. If you question whether you are a controller, my question is, are you sincerely able to wash the feet of your spouse without suppressing her? Are you able to love without making any demands on her?

Owning my story has been a very difficult thing. The shame and the depth of despair and depression I would experience seemed never ending. It felt like I would never be free from the trap and the stench of what I was ensnared with in my family. I felt like I would have to endure this forever.

What I know now about then

Was this dysfunction of control and incest all a part of the picture of what happens in a restrained strict home with spoken and unspoken rules based on tradition? Is the church the cover of security and safety? Disappointedly, my mode of dress did not give me salvation or promise me heaven instead of hell. Nor did the rules of religion give real safety. Is that why it is so easy for the perpetrator to hide behind them? In doing so, they avoid exposure and the fear of what they refuse to control with their own lusts perpetrated on children who have no voice or choice.

Parents have a huge impact on children and shape what the child thinks about themselves and who God is to them. A father in the home is a blueprint for the child's relationship with the Heavenly Father. A relationship with my Heavenly Father was frightening to me as a child, and I still struggled with as an adult. Love was not expressed. There were no hugs. How would I find that in God? As a result, in my thinking, God was far away, harsh, and ready to condemn me. It did not matter what I did; I knew He would disapprove.

In a home with many rules, the child is dominated by their parents with expectations and fear. If Dad is harsh and demanding, the child recoils fearing. Trust is lost. The child sometimes uses manipulation to get around the rules of control, which later as an adult can be followed by controlling others. They follow the pattern of what they learned as a child in a chaotic environment. They may become demanding, attempting to control their environment in order to secure what was so out of control as a child. The wounds of a child carry over into adulthood, and control becomes a way to cope and hide behind. Unless the person is willing to look at the root cause of control, the cycle is passed down to their children.

As a child, one of the saddest things about incest is betrayal. It does not come from your enemies; it comes from your family that you are supposed to trust and be friends with. When the child is at a young age (I was three years old), it is a critical stage of development, of discovering who they are. Sexual abuse is especially difficult as it is beyond their understanding as to "why is this happening?" When men prey on a young child, it is confusing for them. As the survivor child grows older, it can throw them prematurely into adulthood, craving sex but having to suppress those feelings. This especially makes the teenage dating experience difficult.

CHAPTER 9

The incest continued for many years. My brother's sexual gratification happened frequently in the hayloft of the barn on the prickly hay or outside in winter with a bed of snow underneath me. Anywhere, at any time. Sometimes if I felt it was going to happen, I'd try to go another direction, which rarely worked. The whole act disgusted me. I hated the smell after their encounter. I felt so dirty, trapped, and alone in my inside world where the secret was so deep. I did not know or remember when it all started or how to say no to stop it. There was no one to confide in. Somehow it had to be my fault.

Why didn't I tell my mom? I grew up in a family of secrets. We didn't talk about that dirty thing called sex. I was so ashamed about this dark, dark secret that to tell anyone was unthinkable. I did not know how to begin explaining to my mom what my brothers were doing. It was the darkest, most frightening secret. All I knew was I wanted it to go away. My inside world had many walls built thick and high. No one could come into that dark place.

What I was taught at church about sex was that it was a sin before marriage. I was shy and ashamed to my core. The most my mom told me about the reproductive process was, "You should not run at school because you could start bleeding from your private parts." I was confused. A few of my friends educated me. My poor sister was not so fortunate. She started early with her menses, and she thought she was going to die.

At an early age, I believed my dad was to blame for my brother's incestuous behavior. He was their example. Mom alluded that he had an unusual appetite for sex. Little did I recall the extent of what he did to me until I reached my midforties. Was it a truth that I did not remember? I began getting scenes from my past that came to the forefront of my mind like flashes of a memory played out.

In a normal childhood, events create memories. These events go through a part of the brain where they are then stored in the memory banks. When traumatic events happen, it overwhelms the child's brain. They filter the event, and it gets fired off to another part of the brain where it is protected from routine memories. That is a protection for the wellbeing of the child. Frequently, later in one's midthirties to in their fifties, the individual has what are called flashbacks. A flashback is when the visual memory of a past trauma comes up. One sees the surroundings of the event and who is involved in a split second. This can be very confusing unless you are familiar with what is happening. The emotion and the pain of it is real. Soldiers returning from combat often have these flashbacks of traumatic events they went through during combat. Sometimes they remember them and sometimes not.

This happened to me. Out of nowhere, I wondered, where did this thing come from? In the memory/flashback, I was floating above my body, watching the event. Dad was on top of me, having his way sexually. My body was stiff. I saw my eyes fluttering, looking up and to the side, almost like a seizure. Did it happen more than once? The flashbacks of the same scene repeated a few times. Did it happen during the time Mom was in the hospital? I do not know.

The flashbacks were not the full memory for me. Dad died twenty-five years ago, so I could not question him. I knew I had to look at it, much as I did not want to. When I began to explore it, some things suddenly made sense. In one such incident years ago, a friend said something that was very confusing to me. Dad told her he was sorry for what he did to me. I did not understand what she was talking about, even though she knew, but now it made sense.

What I know now about then

I am not grateful for the sexual abuse. How can evil be justified? Hanging Christ on the cross was evil even though good came from it. People in Christian circles are quick to say you have to forgive. Forgiving is important, but healing of the soul takes a process that each person must have the time and freedom to explore. We are too magnificently made to rush this process. Some of my emotions were sadness, grieving the lost years of childhood, as well as anger, and even bitterness. One of the key things I lost was trust. Even trusting God was difficult. How could He allow this to happen to me? As I lost trust, I became fearful. My mind kept racing ahead. I could not look forward without becoming anxious and fearful. My imagination would attempt to maintain control. However, I had to learn to live for just the day I was in much as I did not want to. I learned that my projecting into the future, asking what if, was not real nor of any benefit to me. *"There is no fear in Love, but perfect love casteth out fear: because fear hath torment. He that feareth is not made perfect in love"* (1 John 4:18 KJV) says. I know that God sees the truth of my being and worth because He is love. I am a gift as is every human.

Forgiveness is to let go. It does not mean that I have to socialize with my family. For me, family was not safe. I would never trust my children in their care. Reconciliation means to rebuild trust and the relationship. That can only happen if both parties have forgiven and want to work to rebuild trust.

Back to my story

I had no interest in being anything other than a Mennonite. I did not understand the importance of some of the rules, but the foundation of what the church was built on was what I agreed with, and to think otherwise would be to go against my beliefs. It was the only thing I knew. The rules of the church were my protection from a world that seemed to have no boundaries.

For me, submission meant to respect and obey my elders. When obedience is required, forcing me to give up my will for theirs, resentment and disrespect grows. An example of this was my mom changing from Amish to Mennonite. She did not do it freely. The result was that she disrespected Dad. She did not do it freely. Not being able to express her feelings, she became critical. She found subtle ways to get back at Dad. She resented him, especially when she submitted to what she did not believe in. This is truly what unhealthy submission is—giving in without questions.

The horrible reality of incest did that to me. It insisted that I not resist but passively give in, following my brother's needs. In the end, they had control over me. Control was a pattern that continued throughout my life. In adulthood, I would be attracted to controlling men because that is what I was used to and comfortable with. In relationships, my inner world was unknown to them. My feelings were irrelevant. My lack of identity and worth drove my need to be needed. I became a nurturer—a mom to my mom, a fixer. I was rewarded by appreciation for doing—a worker. It was my salvation and an answer to my out-of-control world. Due to this, I had to determine not to give assent to this. As I learned what God wanted for me, I could establish what He wanted.

Experiencing childhood in normal ways was not my reality. My subservience to my brother's sexual needs would never allow me to speak of it to anyone. Life just happened. I would never have agreed to this misconduct when it was happening. Their rule over me began when I did not have any control over my life. It has been a lifelong process to learn to stand up for myself, giving myself permission to do what is in my best interest.

Later in my marriage, when I was pushed into a corner, I knew that I must take a stand, even if it is most uncomfortable. It would be easier for me to be passive to keep the peace and let life happen. My responsibility was to be pleasing to God first, not man. Christ did not keep the peace. He challenged people to the core. It is an uncomfortable choice, but it gets easier the more I do it. I know I want to be alive and not just exist in life.

I do not believe God ever uses control to accomplish His will over people, although He has control over all things. One of God's greatest gifts to humankind is free will. Even if we make wrong choices and take wrong turns, He is still there for us. He has no illusions about us. That is why Christ was crucified before the earth was formed. It shows me He wants a relationship with us. That is why we were put here. Our response to that is a yearning to worship our Maker, and praise the one who designed us. He responds with delight when we make a choice for Him. He cannot give us direction if we do not move to take an action to choose Him. He desires a relationship with us but never forces it.

I trust that if my free choice is not the best, that He will show me the way and direct me, bringing me closer to Him as the shepherd does when one of His lamb's strays. He takes His rod and gently pulls the lamb back to Himself. That is also the job of the indwelling Holy Spirit to instruct us. He will show me if I ask Him. God is my authority.

Our country's system of government has to do with authority, laws, and power originating from the constitution to control and protect us. A policeman exercises that power to control backed up by the laws of the courts that enforce the policeman's actions. These laws have trickled down to institutions like the workplace, churches, and marriages, to name a few. In Christ's day, the Pharisees tried to trick Him on who His authority was. He asked the Pharisees to show Him a penny in Matthew 22:19 to 21. He asked them whose image was on the penny, and they replied, "Caesar." In verse 21, Jesus replied to them: *"Render therefore unto Caesar the things which are Caesars; and unto God the things which are God's."*

Control has a hold on people. We tend to mix up control with authority. Church leadership has taken the initiative and liberty to make rules or laws according to their interpretation of the Bible. Galatians 3:1–3 talks about the Galatian believers who had been bewitched by the control of the Judaizers who put rules on the people. The Judaizers had justification for their control in their minds. They thought they were acting on behalf of God. *"O foolish Galatians, who hath bewitched you, that ye should not obey the truth, before whose eyes Jesus Christ hath been evidently set forth, crucified among you? This only would I learn of you, Received ye the Spirit by the works of the law, or by the hearing of faith? Are ye so foolish? Having begun in the Spirit, are ye now made perfect by the flesh?* He does not hang the law over us or put us to shame to do all the "shoulds" that well-meaning leaders put before the people, requiring obedience. My question is, "Is it okay if my friend from another organization interrupts the Bible differently? Can I trust God to direct them by His Spirit?"

Satan is always trying to condemn us. Revelation 12:10 says, *"For the accuser of our brethren is cast down, which accused them before our God day and night."* We do not measure up. My response to him is, "And we never will." Remember the verse that says in Romans 8:1, *"There is therefore now no condemnation to them which are in Christ Jesus, who walk not after the flesh but after the Spirit."* Didn't the father run to kiss the wayward prodigal son and put a ring on his finger and a robe on him before celebrating by eating not the skinny but the fat calf?

Back to my story

Dad had another problem. It was Mom. There was no love between them. She was criticized and resented by Dad for as long as I could remember. I would try to reason with him about his complaints concerning her. He complained about her doing things without his approval. Sometimes she did. That made her wrong in his eyes. His solutions to problems were "no." He wanted it done the same way it had always been done. She handled every situation in a different way, which was to help my brothers find their own solutions to problems by looking at all the choices in front of them. She would help them to find their own way. They always referred to her as "the Mom who loved us."

When a dad confides in his child about how bad Mom is, it makes the child feel responsible. If both parents confide in their children, it can cause a battle between the children, which empowers the child to feel important. If a daughter for example is Mom's confidant, the husband often hates his daughter. If the children are too busy caring for their parents, it interferes with their childhood. One of the reasons this is allowed to happen is because there is no closeness or intimacy between Mom and Dad.

I would often feel locked into my inner world. My outside environment was so controlled that I could not feel the deep caverns of sadness underneath. My front was subservient and quiet. My life seemed like a big disappointment. My parents were never able to be there for me. They did the best they knew how with what they were taught. I must find my way. I will not hang onto my failures.

During much of my childhood, I remember Mom being weighed down with life. Frequent headaches were her companion. She would be in bed for what seemed like days. She was overworked and stressed out. She would allude that Dad was after her for more than she wanted to give sexually. I'm not sure Mom forgave him for his infidelity with my aunt Sadie. I believe she resented him on many levels. She was trapped in the relationship.

One of Dad's many complaints were that she was spending too much money buying groceries. On her better days, she would comment to herself that he had enough money to buy his smokes. His smoking was something that the church did not condone. He started this during his young "rumspringa" days in the Amish church and hid it most of the time, especially from his parents. Mom put her foot down and forbade him to smoke in the house.

My parents found it easy to find fault with each other. This is not a spiritual gift, neither it is inspired or led by God. Finding fault is the result of fear, low self-esteem, and anger. It is a futile attempt to end the pain by controlling and forcing others to change. Change does not happen by focusing on the wrong. We change by exposure to God rather than to do faultfinding.

In another incident many years later, Dad's sisters apologized to Mom for encouraging her to marry him. They felt guilty because they wanted him gone, out of the house. He would harass them for sex frequently. He had done this for many years since they were very young. They, too, were trapped by the sexual appetite of an older brother taking advantage of them. No one talked about that secret nor could the girls resist. Later they learned their mother (Grandma) was sexually violated by her older brothers. The open doors of incest were passed down from generation to generation. It has to stop.

At the age of six, my brothers were so proud to let me in on their secrets. There were two things that I could tell no one. The first one was where babies came from. That was disgusting. How could God make such a wrong thing into a baby? And to come out down there. What a disappointment. Every time I saw couples in church that had a baby, I said to myself in disgust, "You did that!" After all, that is what my brothers did to me for as long as I could remember. It was not something a loving husband and wife should do.

The other secret my brothers told me was that we have a half brother. What? What happened? Who? Jake! Does Mom know? You mean I have six brothers now instead of five! Not too much later Mom found out that my brothers had told me, much to her dismay.

Many years later, Mom told me the story about what happened. My oldest brother had just been born. Mom was upstairs nursing him when she heard a commotion downstairs. My aunt Sadie was preparing breakfast. She had been hired to help after my brother's birth. Dad came in from the barn, made a sexual advancement toward her, and they landed on the floor. Mom came downstairs to see what the commotion was about. When she saw what was happening, she fainted and fell down the remainder of the stairs. She became conscious with water being splashed on her face. Dad leaned over her and said, "If you had not refused me this morning, I would not have had to do what I did." She vowed never to refuse him again, no matter what.

As a consequence, nine months later, Sadie had a son out of wedlock, which is my half brother. The Amish bishops came to talk to Dad. He had to confess before the whole church. I wonder, did Aunt Sadie also have to as well since it is mandatory for anyone who indulges in sexual misconduct to go before the church whether you are Amish or Mennonite and confess their sexual sin? In front of the whole church! Shame had to be palpable. Now everyone knows. For Dad, there had to be no joy in knowing his sins were forgiven as he confessed his sin before the church. The experience was degrading, which caused shame from all the congregation and also himself. The shame and the wrong of it was carried with him for the rest of his life, as well as Mom's and Aunt Sadie's lives.

It amazed me in the memoir that my mom wrote many years later that she was most concerned about her little sister. It seemed there was an understanding of the fact that Sadie could not say no. Why was submission at an early age second nature with no ability to resist by saying no or fighting back?

CHAPTER 10

I, being the sixth sibling in the family, was next to the youngest child. It gave me time to develop friendships in the church and neighborhood, unlike my brothers who were older when they left the Amish. I became close friends with two girls both named Ann. We got together on weekends. We would make pizza and invite friends over, sometimes spending the night.

On one occasion, Mom invited the youth group, who were of the same age of my brothers in the church, for a party called a social. My friends and I were allowed to join in. We played some fun games and did folk-type dancing without music since instrumental music was forbidden as worldly. That was short-lived as Mom was gossiped about and criticized by other parents for teaching the young people to dance.

Mom was more of a free spirit. Even though she was brought up in the Amish religion and now was a Mennonite, her values did not always reflect the church rules. My brothers brought home a radio. Not good. The church forbade it. That worldly box of influence would lead one to hell.

My brothers told Mom that our uncle found a radio in one of his sons' cars and smashed it with a hammer in front of them to prove a point. The boys said to themselves if they wanted it, they would have to hide it better, which they did. But not so with Mom. She said, "If you are going to have it, let me listen to it also." She would explore new things before making a judgment. So we'd listen to various shows. Suspense was my favorite. I thought it would be fun to be a crime buster. Dad was passive about it. One day the minister came by to pay us a visit. Mom was funny. She rushed around to hide the radio and put her covering on her head—something she sometimes neglected to do.

Two of Mom's sisters came to visit. They did this every two to three years. Aunt Lydia returned from Africa on furlough when she needed a break as a missionary. She sent postcards informing us of her travels by boat and sometimes by air. I wanted to be like her when I grew up. When I saw an airplane, I wondered if she was on it.

Her other sister Rachel had left the Amish with her family to join the Beachy Amish church, which was more liberal than the Amish. They allowed cars, electricity, and modern farm equipment. Moms' youngest sister Aunt Sadie, still Amish, was not able to visit. That was because of the Amish rule of "shunning," which was meant to separate and isolate our family who were no longer Amish, so she could not associate with us.

Mom would laugh, which was rare for her, when they came. There was a camaraderie among them. They acted like they were in their teens. Teasing and pulling pranks was a large part of the fun. It was fun to watch. One of the downers for me was when Aunt Rachel laughingly teased Irma and me. We had small kittens, and she would threaten both of us by holding them by the head and threatening to twist off their heads. Even though I doubted she would actually do it, I still questioned whether she would. We begged her not to.

One day news came that Mom's youngest sister, Aunt Sadie, and her family were moving to Michigan. Even though Aunt Sadie had a son out of wedlock (my half brother), she found a husband, and they got married in the Amish church. We would go to their house after dinner and play games such as hide-and-seek in the back yard with my cousins while the adults played cards. It was fun until my aunt Sadie's husband grabbed me on two occasions and took me to the wash house. There his oldest daughter was laughing and chuckling at the other end of the room while he fondled me. I was confused and embarrassed. I could not get away from his grip nor resist. I was glad they were moving.

BEHIND THE SCENE

Continuing on with my story

At nine years old, there was a preacher who came to our town, and many of the churches supported him as he would hold revival meetings in a large tent, which he put up in a field. We would go almost every evening. After the service I would see ministers surrounding my dad and mom. They were talking to Dad to get him to accept Jesus in his heart. He would resist and became increasingly more angry and sullen as the evenings went on.

I asked my mom what people were doing who went upfront during the altar call at the end of the service and if it would be okay for me to go. She said it was. So the next evening, I braved it. I was so scared as I walked forward, not knowing what to expect. They ushered us to the back where a gentleman sat with an empty chair next to him. As I was directed to sit next to him, he explained what John 3:16 was about. I said the prayer that he asked me to repeat after him, and I felt the weight of the world lift off my shoulders. I was free. They asked if I wanted to give my testimony in the front of the tent full of people, and I agreed. I told them that I was free, and God had forgiven my sins. I had never experienced such peace with a freedom that made me unafraid.

Then I went home, and the realization hit me. *How long could I be free?* I wondered. I was subject to my brothers. I did not know how to resist. Would God forgive me, and would He take away the peace I had found? Unfortunately, after a week, there was no answer to what I was faced with in my family. *Please, God, help me and forgive me.*

I was trapped and shut down. I did not realize until I became an adult and had my own children that the blame that I put on myself for what happened was wrong. I was just a child. Hating ourselves, my sister and I shared the same low self-worth, shame, and fear of exposure of our inside world. We did not discuss it, but we both knew what the other was subjected to. She experienced incest by four out of five of my brothers. Her self-worth was nonexistent.

One of my brothers would try to pimp me out to my half brother, Jake, when our families would get-together. He would bribe me with candy and beg me as he herded me away from the group of cousins that I was playing games with. I'd resist and run away. Good for me! During this time, he also persisted by bringing the teenage neighbor boys to our farm and they would beg me again, but to no avail. I resisted.

When I was ten years, old my oldest brother got married. Mom wanted me to go visit him and his wife in a city a few hours away. I did not want to go. Would he leave me alone? The morning came when his wife left to teach school, and we were alone for a brief time. With a sigh of relief, I can say he did not touch me. However, I was not comfortable being around him, especially alone.

There was a lot of change in the next few years. It was exciting and frightening. My one-room country school was closing. When I was thirteen, my brother Ruben, my sister Irma, and myself were headed for public school in town. The old dirt road that ran in front of our house closed and a single lane road was carved out through the neighbor's field connecting our house to the main road below. The new road would be graveled. The bus would stop to pick us up.

Middle school does not have fond memories for me. On one occasion, the teenage neighbor that my brother had brought to our farm to bribe me threatened to tell all my classmates what he knew about my brothers and me. I felt like my life was over. The whole world would know what I was so desperate to protect. I was relieved that no one ever teased me or told me that they knew anything of my secret. The only harassment I got was on the bus every evening, one of the boys would tell me that I would never amount to anything. I had few friends. I was not comfortable being me. Children at school picked up on my insecurities. They would shy away from being my friend. However, there were a few smart ones whom I could talk to when I had questions about schoolwork. I liked them. They did not care about popularity.

One morning I woke up to see Mom looking out the window and crying. Going down the old dirt road that had not been traveled on for years were two of my brothers walking with their bags slung over their shoulders. They were restless. Mom helped them pack even though she did not agree. Indiana had promises of a better life with jobs and more young people. Some would say they ran away from home. Or did they just decide to try something different? It was sad to see them go. Little did we know how difficult it would be for them. They disclosed to Mom years later that at times they slept in their cars in the winter with holes in their shoes and very little to eat. With them gone, I began to realize that I was free from further sexual harassment. I was free!

CHAPTER 11

As for me I followed the traditions of the church. At twelve years old, my friend, whom I will call Ann, and I wanted to join the Mennonite church and be baptized. When we were baptized, we went before the church; and as we knelt, the minister poured water on our heads from a cup. It was an exciting new chapter in my life, and I looked forward to becoming a part of the church. The requirement was to attend classes to learn the ordinances passed down from the Anabaptists, as well as numerous restrictions enforced by the church leadership. An important one was how to dress modestly. I was old enough to wear a dress with a cape to church.

A cape was an extra material covering over the woman's bodice of her dress to hide her curvature. My question during instruction class was, "If the men were going to look at my curvatures on Sundays, they could also on weekdays when we were not required to wear them. Why is it so important?" I asked.

The pastor said, "It would keep the men from lusting after you."

Then I asked, "Why do I have to cover my womanhood to protect the inability of the men to govern their own thoughts?"

He responded, "The women are responsible to not cause anyone to stumble or lead the men in the wrong direction."

I was happy to wear it even though it did not make a lot of sense to me. I wore my maroon dress repeatedly. It was the only one I had.

BEHIND THE SCENE

Today in the same church, there are no capes worn, and I asked, "What changed? Was it well intended to keep us in line with the organization's rules to protect us from all the temptations of the world?"

I believe it is important to dress modestly and appropriately for different situations. However, it is more important for me to be a light of who God is in me first, and the dress will follow. When I see people in society dress seductively, I wonder why they dress that way. It does not make me want to be like them.

Are women partially responsible? I believe so. I have seen where women have made it difficult for men to resist them. Men are naturally the pursuers. That is the way God made us. My friend would tell me, "Men seduce with their words, and women seduce with their bodies." There is a lot of wisdom in that statement.

When I was sixteen years old, I went to a Winter Bible college in Ohio for a six-week session. I did this every year for three years. The third year, I graduated. While there, I had an interesting experience. One of my roommates noticed that I had shaved my legs. (In more conservative circles, women do not shave their legs). She asked me one day, "If Christ returned, would you want to be shaving your legs?" She was implying that I had vanity and should not be doing it. Of course, I would be ashamed and would not want that! Years later, as I thought about it, I said to myself, if I were going to the bathroom, that would not be a good time for Him to return either! A light bulb went off in my head. This had to be a false shame. Or in God's eyes, is it shameful at all?

I am saved by grace; I desire to be like Him. When God sees me, He sees the one that He made like himself, in His image, that Christ bought by redeeming me. Was Jesus dying on the cross enough to cover my sin? A teacher once asked me, "Or is your sin so bad that He needs to do it again?" That means I am dead to sin. He also said, "When God looks at us, He is not looking at what is wrong with us, but He sees what we are missing as a believer and works to correct that." God challenges me in the area of my greatest needs. So instead of me asking why this happened to me, I ask, "What is it that I didn't know before this that You would like for me to know? What is it that you were not able to be in me that you want to be now?"

Sin means to miss the mark. In the Old Testament, the Jews interpreted sin as that which is not perfect. So if I am on the wrong path, I have a choice to take another direction. It is my choice; I trust He will lead me. His shed blood was enough to cleanse me. I do not have to help Him. There is nothing I can do that adds to my salvation. He gave it to me. I love Him, and I do not want to displease Him. That is the difference. I am worthy of being loved. His intention is for me to be whole. I get that, as God wants to have a relationship with me as a mature daughter. There is nothing I can do that will make Him love me less or more.

Leaders in the church continued to preach on what the rules of the church were. If the people did not follow, then they experienced guilt, shame, and the fear of hell. Was their concern more about the rules than salvation? Today this seems like a way to control. The Bible was drilled into my head, condemning and placing guilt on me if I didn't do it right. Today I realize that many times, doctrine taken from the Bible and interpreted a certain way creates a culture where people accept what is taught as the truth. It totally bypasses the true meaning of who Christ is when we have a relationship with Him. The church is to represent Christ freeing me from the law. *"Blotting out the handwriting of ordinances that was against us, which was contrary to us, and took it out of the way, nailing it to the cross"* Colossians 2:14 (KJV) says.

The rules of the church stated that the women's hair part was to be down the middle of the head. During my teen years, I loved doing different things with my hair. I'd put waves on the front part of my hair in front of my covering and do a side part. My friends and other youth did the same hair part during the week. They chose to comb their hair to a center part on Sundays when attending church. I was not going to be a hypocrite. In my mind I would rationalize, justifying what I was doing. If I did it during the week, I was not going to change it for Sunday.

Much to my dismay, I received a letter in the mail requesting that I change my ways. Parting my hair in the middle was the rule, and if I continued to disobey, then excommunication from the fellowship would be considered. It came as a shock; and I felt sad, embarrassed, and hurt. I didn't want to be anything but a part of the church. Why would they not talk to me first? How do these restrictions make me a more spiritual person?

Sometimes their response would be, "Well, that is just how we do it," or "If we allow one rule to be compromised, it will open the door to allow more liberties which is worldly." That was a thing to be feared. I followed the progression of their thoughts that opening one door could cause more change to occur. The Church frowned on change as a good thing. That was a frightening risk to become more like the world.

Rules did not get me closer to Jesus. My relationship with Him is not rewarded by the amount of work I do or rules I follow. Today Jesus dying on the cross was enough for me to be redeemed. I'm free from the law of sin and death. He did away with it. "He filled me to all the fullness." My greatest delight and challenge in life is to stay close to Him. He makes me righteous. *"The Lord your God in your midst of thee, is Mighty; he will save, He will rejoice over you with joy, He will rest in His love, He will rejoice over you with singing"* (Zephaniah 3:17 KJV), and, *"I do not set aside the grace of God, for if righteousness comes through the law then Christ died in vain"* (Galatians 2:21 KJV). And one more from the apostle Paul, *"For he is not a Jew, which is one outwardly; neither is that circumcision, which is outward in the flesh: But he is a Jew, which is one inwardly and circumcision is that of the heart, in the spirit, and not in the letter; whose praise is not of men, but of God"* (Romans 2:28–29 KJV).

A wise teacher once told me, "God loves people more than the rules." One of my favorite examples of this was when the Jews brought the prostitute to Jesus, saying that she was caught in the act of adultery. The law, which was called the Torah, says to stone her. She needed only two witnesses to condemn her. Jesus states in John 8:7, *"He that is without sin among you, Let him cast a stone first."* All her accusers left because no one was guiltless to pick up one stone. Jesus was the only one there who could condemn her. The Torah states that the one being condemned needed two witnesses. Jesus, being one person, said to her, *"Go and sin no more."* That is His yoke. He says it is easy. I believe God wants us back in relationship with Him more than paying us back for the wrong we did. This is who He is.

CHAPTER 12

Dad never wanted us to go to school more than was required by the state, which was the eighth grade. His Amish roots did not escape him. My brothers all stopped school at eighth grade except my oldest brother who went on to college to become a minister. People at church told me I was different from the others in my family. I reminded them that I came from the same batch. I would fight anger at their rejection of my family and couldn't bear leaving anyone out. However, I vowed that I would go further in school.

When it came time for me to go to high school, there were two options—the Mennonite high school, which was too expensive for my family; or the public school, which was not encouraged by the church or done by many of the Mennonite young people. I followed the tradition of what Mom did by going to work for families with newborn babies. I absolutely hated it. I washed cloth diapers and helped with many chores on their farms, including milking the cows. The money I made went to my parents. That is what Dad expected.

I have grieved over my sister, Irma, many times with deep regret. What more could I have done for her? She used humor to cope with her struggles and rarely talked about her disappointments. She took life as it came and made the best of it. She never connected with anyone as friends within the church. Her friends were on the fringes of a different, more conservative church called the Beachy Amish.

As a teenager, Irma was considered by our church as the black sheep of the family, as were most of my brothers. She did not see the importance of the traditions of the church with all the rules that the church thought was important. She explored other avenues. Playing with hair was her creative flare. She wanted to become a hairdresser, but that was forbidden by the church. She had no money to pursue what she wanted to do, all the while questioning if her disobedience to the church was a bad thing that would doom her to hell. She did other secondary jobs, never finding her way to her passion.

She fell in love at a young age with one of the young men from the Beachy Amish church, who by that time had left that church. After dating for a short while, he broke off the relationship. Irma, because of a broken heart, became more and more depressed. One late evening coming home from work, she was awake and rather giddy, laughing and telling me funny things. This caught my attention as it was not characteristic of her at that time because of her breakup. I pressured her to find out what changed. I saw she was not doing well. She looked pale and began vomiting. She finally confessed that she took a bottle of Tylenol. I woke up Mom, and she was rushed to the hospital. She nearly destroyed her liver. After her hospitalization, she went into rehabilitation. I learned later when suicide is contemplated that one of the stages before it is implemented is they get happy and giddy. Their decision to end the turmoil in their minds is freeing for them.

A few years later, Johnny who had returned from Indiana, also wrote a suicide note. His fiancée broke off the relationship with him. I came home from being out with friends and saw he was writing what seemed to be an agonizing letter to someone. He seemed depressed, not wanting to talk. My questioning him did not result in a satisfactory answer. I stayed up trying to encourage him. That fell to the ground. Something was not right. Before he left, he went to put the letter under Mom and Dad's bedroom door and instead asked if I would have Mom read it in the morning. He then left the house and was planning on hanging himself at the farm where he was working some thirty miles away.

I did not hesitate to wake up Mom to open the envelope after he left. I then called the police who intercepted him on the road to his workplace. Mom, Dad, and our neighbor who was a Christian counselor went to meet Johnny at the police station. Mom said Johnny began sobbing when he saw them, saying he did not want to do it. He went into counseling after that incident.

Johnny nor my sister tried it again. I do think suicide is a real thing to be aware of especially as teenagers are trying to find their way in life and their life looks hopeless and their self-esteem for whatever reason is nonexistent.

Irma got married at nineteen to the man who had broken her heart earlier. They were not a part of any church group. She worked at difficult jobs, such as cooking at restaurants. Her husband left her when their son was young. Breathing in the rancid fumes of fast-food cooking and smoking took her to an early death.

CHAPTER 13

Survivors of sexual abuse who are in their teen years have difficulty putting down boundaries while exploring relationships. What is meant to be healthy boundaries is compromised. It is a difficult struggle. It is difficult enough for those who have not been violated to figure it out. Many teenagers become flirtatious, looking for the attention of the opposite sex; this is normal. Dress becomes important to be attractive. Many times, it is difficult to know what is appropriate. Sometimes the flirtations or interest shown are read by the opposite sex as an invitation to be preyed on.

This is confusing to the survivor because it is as though an invisible mark has been put on them. It is an unspoken gateway that men sense and can take advantage of. This happened to me on a first date. I was surprised at his advances, and I was firm that my body was off-limits. He said, "I am surprised!" His comment was confusing to me. I had done nothing to encourage his aggression. What a big disappointment that anyone would think I would condone his actions.

Instead of being flirtatious, the survivor sometimes has the opposite reaction. Their loose-fitting clothes shows their low self-esteem. They do not want boys to be attracted to them. Others around them respond by questioning their worth as well. Self-acceptance is crucial for them but difficult to find or believe in. In addition, survivors sometimes cling to those they love, unable to tolerate a healthy level of independence. Or they may become too absorbed in their problems to pay attention to anyone else.

How do I receive or give nurturing? Physical closeness can be threatening and confusing. It was easier to establish closeness with friends than with potential lovers. Then there are times when survivors sexualize every friendship, then run away when intimacy enters the picture. Or one may start to get more involved in the relationship, and when it starts to feel like the family who hurt you, you panic. It is tough to give or receive love.

When I was a teenager, I'd go into total anxiety if there was a hint of a deeper connection with anyone of the opposite sex. It is hard to explain how severe it is. I was able to divert my pain by being shy. Or I would be over-the-top boisterous and inappropriate all the while feeling inadequate, covering up my pain.

Religion was my protection and a shell in which I hid. The rules and adherence to the dress code, however, did not protect me, my sister, nor my parents, even though they were taught over the pulpit every year. It restrained and suppressed me, insisting that I submit. Looking back, I asked myself, "Was that their way to control us?"

I have watched when restraints are put on a group of people by insisting adherence to their rules. Unhealthy behaviors then can come to the surface. People do not acknowledge that they have the freedom to have their own thoughts to process what is right and wrong. The rules that are supposed to protect them, sadly impose unhealthy restraints, which allow people to hide behind the rules and avoid exposure.

This pattern of hiding sexual sin for my family was carried down through multiple generations. The Bible tells us that the sins of the fathers are passed down through many generations. Did these sins become a part of my DNA? Is this why it was happening repeatedly? It may not look the same in the next generation as it was for me, but it can manifest in other sexual misconduct.

Eventually we moved off the farm into town. I decided to go to correspondence school to get my high school diploma. I wanted to become a nurse. I knew that I cared about people who needed help. I started by applying at the senior home care facility for a nurse's aide job. They accepted me when I was almost sixteen years old. The administrator would encourage me by saying, "You can do this." I took courses relating to my job, learning how to give personal care for the elderly residents, whom I loved. Working at the nursing home was a wonderful positive experience. Each person had a unique personality. I loved working with my friends from church who also worked there, as well as making new friends. Ultimately, I was given the great responsibility of being the only nurse on the night shift, caring for the fifty residents.

Dad again insisted that my wages be paid to him, but this time I refused to allow him to have it. I did not see any improvements from my previous wages given to him, so I assumed that he wasted it. I insisted that I manage my money; however, I used it to pay the numerous bills my parents had accrued through the years. There were countless doctor and hospital bills. Consistently every month, I would send money for the various bills until my parents were debt-free.

Needless to say, it still angered my dad a great deal because he did not have control. After all, control was very important because of the way he had been taught. If there was no control, his authority was challenged as the head of the house. It brought up all kinds of insecurities, which was very unsettling for him. His demeanor was silent, angry. His moodiness and pouting made everyone uncomfortable.

Throughout my life, I have repeatedly learned how abusive control works, although at first, I did not recognize or call it that. I would find myself in situations repeatedly that were difficult to get out of. To this day, God is still increasing my awareness and approach by responding when the incident is occurring instead of pulling back and allowing it to happen. It is easier for me to recognize abusive control because I am getting better at identifying and confronting situations by not allowing them to scar me or wound any part of me.

I returned a second year to Winter Bible School in Ohio with some of my girlfriends. It was always an exciting and challenging experience. Studying about Bible times and getting closer to Jesus was what I loved.

I dated a few guys but nothing very serious. My boundaries were in place at Bible school and at home during my teens and into my twenties. I chose to be virtuous.

When I returned home from Bible school the realization hit me that the rules for sexual sin by the church were that one had to make a public confession before the congregation no matter if it was current or in the past. If the leaders of the church knew, what would be required of me? What would be done about it? What if my brothers, who were already marginalized in the church, were humiliated or worse, thrown out of the church, further isolating them? Would the ministers protect me by not exposing my sin to the church? Even my own silence felt better than any of that.

I recall young couples going to the front of the church and confessing their sexual transgressions. People would pass judgment, gossiping and wrapping them in shame for many years. They were sentenced to always remember their sin. I felt like my reputation and life would be ruined, also my brothers if I confessed. I was confident that Christ loved me and did not want me to feel the shame and the power that bondage held over me. Unfortunately, I could not see the stigma lifted off the couples that had confessed nor was it forgotten by others.

I knew if I confessed, not only my reputation but what little reputation my family had would be destroyed. Really, God, must I confess? I hit a crisis! At night I would take the car and drive for what seemed like hours. Then I'd take walks. I cried out, "God, help me!" Even though I knew God's love, I struggled with depression and worthlessness, and I withdrew from others. After a month of crying out to God, hoping for some kind of answer, He clearly answered me, "The rules of the church are not My requirements. Your sin is what I died for." Wow, that made so much sense. There was a higher government that did not support what the church required. I could continue to walk and grow with Him knowing He loved me unconditionally and knowing He did not desire to have me shamed or punished in this anymore!

During this time, I learned the value of a friend through my close friend whom I will call Ann. She never turned her back on me even though I withdrew from friends. I thank God for her as she never rejected me as a friend. To this day, we are still close friends. She had no idea of what my inside world was about. We were always searching for more spiritually. We separated later when we went to different colleges.

My ambition was to be a nurse and a missionary. I moved to Michigan to go to nursing school. Upon completion, I was preparing to go to the mission field in Central America when I became very unsettled in my heart. I had three months to prepare. How was I going to help the people? I would help them medically by giving medications and teaching them good hygiene. The important goal was salvation. But what after that? Would I be persuading them on the rules of the church? Or was the history of the Mennonites a foundation that was important for them to learn? Did they need to follow my ways as a Mennonite, especially in my manner of dress? I had salvation, but where were the power and miracles that the church had in Acts? Were the prophets all dead? The verse that Christ says in John 14:12, *"He that believeth on me, the works that I do shall he do also; and Greater works than these shall he do; because I go unto my Father."* What did that mean? All I knew was that I didn't have what the Bible was talking about, nor did I want to make excuses to the people for what I didn't see God being or doing today. I was on a quest to find answers. The Bible colleges in the area did not have classes available within the time frame that I was looking for. I had only three months before my departure date to the mission field.

Out of the blue, my cousin, whom I will call Susan, called me. She said, "I have found what we have been looking for!" Then she added, "I am moving to the West Coast to learn more about this church. I can send you some tapes of their teaching." Every spare minute I had for the next three weeks, I would listen to the teaching tapes that Susan sent me. They taught that the foundation of the church was the apostles, prophets, evangelists, pastors, and teachers. The Holy Spirit was an important part of their walk with God. Who was the Holy Spirit? I wanted to know more. So when she asked me to go along with her and drive, I agreed. Admittedly I was afraid, but I agreed to go for a month.

My roommate listened to the teachings also and insisted that she wanted to go too. She wanted to take her car. Things fell into place rapidly. I sold my car within a week, packed up my clothes, and we were on our way in two weeks. I reassured the pastor at my Mennonite church that I would return to go to Central America. The pastor was visibly upset. I asked for a month to do research on this spiritual movement that was happening, then I would return. He said, "You will not be back."

I loved the people in my small church, and sadly I responded that I just needed to find some answers, then I would return. Before I left, he would imply in his sermons that what I was searching for was misguided. One of my questions was, are the prophets of today really dead? Where is the power of the apostles as in the New Testament? Why were miracles infrequent?

We drove to Iowa to pick up Susan, and the three of us were on our way to the West Coast. Money was limited. We would drive straight through without stopping overnight. I witnessed my first miracle on the long trip there.

The snowstorm that blanketed the Midwest made the roads all but impassable. News reports were telling people not to drive. The gas station attendant warned us to please not go farther. We saw trucks and cars in the ditch as we traveled along. I prided myself in being experienced in navigating in the snow, but this was a serious situation. We started to worship, trusting we were following what God wanted. The roads started to clear, and the snow stopped. The other girls would then go to sleep. I was used to working nights, so I continued to drive as the others slept. Within a few hours, the snow started again packing the roads with limited visibility, demanding my full attention. I woke up the girls, and we again began to worship. Again, the snow stopped, and the roads cleared. This pattern went on the whole night.

When at last we arrived, we were well taken care of. The people in the church were accepting, and I learned a lot. I read and studied. I also did my own form of "rumspringa." I did not wear my cape. I noticed that there was no change in the way people related to me. I am grateful that I had someone who was like a dad to me who kept track of me. He would say, "If you do this, the result will be that." Or "How will the decision you are going to make affect your relationship with God?"

He kept speaking the truth to me of who I am without putting a restraint on me by giving me choices. All the while I was growing spiritually and learning. He told me the pendulum of what I did would swing extremely to the far right, but I would learn moderation, which would bring it back to the middle. I knew in my gut it was not the rules in my head that I had been taught but the importance of what brought me closer to commune with my Heavenly Father. He filled me with His Holy Spirit. This gave me a new freedom as I continued to open my heart more to God.

After living in California and being exposed to this new teaching, I realized after only three weeks that I could not return to be a Mennonite or go to the mission field as a Mennonite. What I learned in the Bible that had become real to me would not align with the Mennonite teaching. At the age of twenty-four, I wrote to my pastor (whom I love and respect to this day) a letter stating that what I had learned was not under the approved umbrella of the Mennonite church. Very sadly I asked him, "Please find someone else to replace me."

Facing the unknown had no safety. My mind was used to the routine along with the rules of my comfortable way of thinking, including the familiarity of my relationships with family and the church. The enormity of the change for me tempted me to fear the unknown. But instead, I decided to trust God, face the unknown by leaning on Him. Often people shrink back believing there are no other options for them. It then becomes easier to fall back to old ways of thinking, and unfortunately one often wonders later, "What if I had chosen a different direction that was open for me, how would my life be different?" This is paralyzing as there is no answer to those questions that kept repeating themselves.

Before going to California, I came to what is called a spiritual crisis. My indecision did not feel comfortable, but in retrospect, the decision to go was the right decision. What I had in my spiritual walk was not enough for me in my search. Often this happens more than once in a person's life. Some have even called it a "dark night of the soul," especially when there are no obvious answers or open doors to go through. Jesus said in Luke 11:9, *"And I say unto you, Ask, and it shall be given you: seek and ye shall find: knock, and it shall be opened unto you."* I would ask God to open doors to find more of Him. Sometimes in my impatience, it seemed to take a long time. When that door opens, it is usually unfamiliar, frightening, and sometimes exciting at the same time. I ask God to give me confirmation on my decision. I had no idea of the outcome, but I had to take the first step. I had to turn in a different direction. What I learned was life changing, freeing my thinking, and embracing uncertainty by releasing the traditional hold that my religious ways had on me. One of the important things that I learned is that repentance means more than what I was taught.

When King James translated the Bible to English, he used the word *repentance* for the Greek word *metanoia*. *Meta* means to change or go further, and *noia* is our mind. This change of mind meant that I would have to look at and let go of the perception I had of everything. This process was one of letting go of my old ways of thinking by embracing and trusting God in the uncertainty those changes brought.

In the middle of a trial, great faith is not the absence of doubt. Great faith is a trust in the middle of the storm that keeps moving forward as my heart stays clean and pure.

Paul writes, *"But now we are delivered from the law, that being dead wherein we were held; that we should serve in newness of spirit and not in the oldness of the letter"* (Romans 7:6 KJV). Stepping away from the security of the law *was* scary for me. This freedom put the responsibility back on me by openly embracing uncertainty as I walk in faith. My choices are important to honor God and myself. With this newfound insight came the responsibility to walk in God's consciousness every day not enslaved by the set law that I had hoped would give me salvation.

The fear of being wrong is another kind of fear. Our Father holds no record of a wrong. If I ask, He will guide me to *all* truth the Bible says, which He called the Spirit of Truth. This truth and love go together, assuring us that we belong to Him. Truly, darkness is the culprit that blinds us by keeping us from knowing how much our Father loves us. His grace requires nothing in return for this favor.

We cannot claim to have done it right to earn this grace for our salvation.

Love removes fear. Some of our fears are that we will not be enough or that because of our own uncertainty of doing what we are not comfortable with we will suffer loss. I found this in the changes that I now embraced.

Leaders of churches often fear losing control of people because it is difficult to trust the choices people make. I understand this because as a parent, my teen and adult children made choices that I believed were to their detriment. As difficult as it is, I have to stand by and watch, praying for God to bring His wisdom to them. I could not stop them unless of course it was life-threatening. In medicine, there is frequently more than one treatment to get to the desired healing outcome for the patient. It is the same in life. Choice and the process of problem-solving allows them to grow as a person. If they need my help, they will ask for it. The important thing I believe is to be there for them with grace, love, and encouragement, which allows them to grow. Christ to me is this example.

Can religion have a relationship when it is used as a weapon? Religion convinces oneself by doing. It is a god that does not exist. It enforces mistruths that we believe about ourselves. God has already accepted you in His life. John 12:32 says, "And *I, If I be lifted up from the earth, will draw all man unto Me.*" God is in love with us. We think He is distant, which makes us have to work to earn our salvation.

Religion introduces many "shrouds." For me it was a feeling that I must do things to be worthy of Him or have the approval of the church. If I did not read the word enough or take the time to sit in silence to pray or commune with Him, then in my mind, I was flawed. I had to work to show myself approved by God. I could not trust God for His approval. If I could not trust my earthly father, then how could I trust my Heavenly Father?

People will disagree. This doesn't make their truth something I have to follow. Seeking the truth is my responsibility. When I share a thought or action that is different, it can be just as unifying as when everyone agrees perfectly with each other.

However, I believe it is important to agree with each other in prayer to see a matter resolved. Matthew 18:19 says, *"Again I say unto you, that if two of you shall agree on earth as touching anything that they shall ask, it shall be done for them of my Father which is in heaven."*

CHAPTER 14

One day many years later, my cousin Susan called me again. This time she brought up *the subject*. She said, "You will not be a whole person until you look at the abuse that happened to you as a child." She was one of the few who knew about the incest. I tossed it aside, refusing to look at what I had determined to leave behind me. The past was the past. I had no time to think of such dark things, and eventually, I believed I would forget it. My life was full of good things that would offset the bad that had happened in the past. I was a busy wife and mother, helping my husband with his career, as well as being heavily involved in our church as a pastor's wife. However, in my heart, I knew I was not free. Now in my midforties, I began to wonder if my past was still haunting me. I started to take an honest look at what was going on inside of me. At times I still felt inferior, insecure, and unworthy, with many negative thoughts about myself. They would come out of nowhere or could be triggered after a comment in a conversation with someone.

I found myself gravitating to books on healing from abuse, and I knew deep down that I wanted to discuss it with someone. The words on the pages would jump off at me. For example, sentences like, "The family's sexual secrets that are kept hidden are bound to repeat themselves in the next generations." Families have difficulty addressing these needs. I vowed to myself that I would not pass any unhealed areas on to my children. Sadly, I had neither taken the time to heal, nor would I acknowledge the trauma that I had experienced.

I got to the place where I wanted to be free of the torment of my past by letting go of the old cycles in my mind that kept circulating and bubbling to the surface. I experienced emptiness that was not satisfied with accomplishments. I even tried long hours at work. I felt isolated, fighting to believe I was good enough, especially for God. In my quest to be perfect, I would always evaluate whether I was pleasing God, which included judging myself and others. I always came up lacking.

I needed to take the risk of exposure to talk to a counselor. In other words, I was done with the secrets. No matter how disgusting it was or how much I hated to pull up my memories and go into the depth of it, I needed to be free of the secret package that I protected for so long.

One of the most frightening things for me was to face the incest all by myself. I knew this would be challenging for my husband and family even if I did not share the details. Would I be discarded by my husband? I had so many fears and questions. When would I know that I have been healed completely? Would I be able to be intimate to trust? How do I talk to my husband, and would he understand or dismiss it as not important since it happened so long ago? I felt so unclean and isolated. It seemed like an old life from another time. What if it was my fault? Would it require endless time and money, which I didn't have? Do I have to confront my abusers? My struggles were deep. Under my desire of growing spiritually, going to school, working, and being a good wife in support of my husband and children, there was still a broken person who fought a sense of failure. I'd fake it till I'd make it, right? Wrong.

For the unhealed, incest is a forever torment that alienates one in aloneness. It desecrates and destroys you from your heart. It is an imbalance of power of someone older in the family who preys on a younger child for sexual gratification. Incest breeds needy relationships.

As a teenager, one is looking for someone in misguided love to fill in the dark holes that were created through the act of incest. Some become promiscuous because they are looking to fill those holes. One hides their insecurity in hopes that it will go away, which it never does for the unhealed. In the instability of the broken heart, relationships flounder, and self-esteem is under attack. Yet again you face your own vulnerability by being less than, believing that you are not worthy of being loved.

Incest is one of those things you wish would just magically go away. Emotional boundaries are nonexistent. One can feel totally alone, numb, and in agony. The painful memories I had were an emotional roller coaster. Trust fluctuates between no trust to complete trust. Rejection of oneself and from others is always hiding, ready to surface at any time. There is no understanding what healthy love is because the example of what should have been love is flawed, making the person believe they are unlovable. Survivors of abuse can be afraid they will abuse their children in some way. Some choose to have no children because of this. Being afraid is okay. Acting out is not. Once you have done your healing, it is unlikely you will abuse.

It was a tough process for me to find a good therapist. I interviewed a few. Ideally, I wanted someone who had recovered from abuse so that I could feel safe to talk freely. Not many in my area had experienced sexual abuse. I found this period incredibly difficult as I was baring my soul to what I had never been willing to discuss. Eventually I did find a therapist, but I would walk out of the sessions feeling like dirt. He would say, "Until you get it out and deal with it, it will come back to haunt you. It will trip you up later." I decided to trust what my gut told me and what the therapist said.

The process of feeling what I did not feel as a child was a dark experience. There was no one I could talk to or trust as I relived the past. Most people around me did not know how to relate to me. Once I attempted to share with a woman who led a twelve-step healing group from a different church, but she would recoil as if I was damaged goods. My pastors did not want me to relive it. Even well-meaning brothers or sisters in the church missed the truth of what I was doing to get my healing. I soon learned not to discuss it with anyone but my therapist. I learned that trust had to be earned. It did not come automatically.

Another time my counselor reluctantly gave me permission to talk to a close, trusted friend who pressured me to know what I was doing. He said, "It needs to be one who will listen and not judge or gossip about it to others." I felt confident that my friend would do that. A few weeks later, I was horrified to learn that many people knew. She apologized, however, justifying it to me by saying she told "only one person," but that person told many friends. In this I learned that it is too much information for most people to handle. When they do not know how to process it, they feel like they need to tell someone. Some other well-meaning friends gave advice that was confusing to me. What I truly wanted was to have someone sit by my side supporting me without my needing to talk. This was a big setback for me. In the midst of my vulnerability and insecurities, I lost trust, and my wounds were even more exposed and raw.

My therapist would encourage me to journal my thoughts, especially when I got anxious. Writing out my feelings allowed me to say what I wanted even though it was difficult to give myself permission to feel my feelings. There was such anger, along with a deep sadness because of the loss and grief. The shame of it never allowed me to get close to anyone during this time.

These are a few notes from my journaling. If I feel and believe that I am worth nothing, I will act like "a nothing." When my secrets are covered over, they become dark. In exposing my secrets to light, I take the risk that God is good, but I also take the risk that what if He is not? Until I believe that God is good, how can I trust Him? Sometimes God has been presented to me as strict, angry, and austere who is disapproving and disappointed in people like me. The truth is really that His fury is for me, not against me. Fury to destroy a wrong done to me. He does not need me or anyone. He is complete in Himself. I am not powerful enough to separate myself from God's love. Christ does not run from my suffering, nor did He run from His. He carried it to His Gethsemane. I found Him in my darkness, committed to my deepest wound. Pain had a way of clipping my wings even though I knew He meant for me to be free. He is the one who tells me who I am. Being made in His image, I have my own keynote signature of worship and fragrance that He identifies as me.

I continued to learn more. Parents from a dysfunctional family have difficulty establishing their child's value. Children born into these families have needs that cannot be met. They are needy, imperfect, immature, vulnerable, and valuable. In God's kingdom, children get their needs met. When living in a dysfunctional family, one cannot address these needs. The innocence of the child is taken away. The tendency is to force them to be perfect on the outside by adhering to the rules. This is managing them from the outside in. This sets up low self-esteem, making them feel like they are not valuable. The child, instead of a "human being" learns to become a "human doing," always working in order to feel good about themselves. With this dysfunction, they put other people on a pedestal as better than themselves. That was me.

As a wife, I put my husband's wishes above mine, especially due to the teaching of submission in the church. I justified it because I believed the woman was made for the man. With time, this devalues the woman for who she is making it difficult for her to express or have her own opinion. Underneath this giving up of my opinion to another's grows a hatred of the woman by either sex. I did not like myself nor appreciate other women in my circle. This hatred is called misogyny.

I told my children of my abuse, explaining what happened to me and how it changed my life and could affect theirs if they are not aware. I taught them early that if anyone ever touched them in areas that are not appropriate, they were to say no and to tell me immediately. I informed them that sometimes the perpetrator threatens to harm someone in the family if they tell. I will not condemn them but protect them. I am cautious when there are sleepovers at peoples' homes as well as social events or playing hide-and-seek after dark. I am not fearful but aware. Many times, the abuser threatens the child that if you tell anyone, there will be consequences. Another is if you don't tell, I will reward you.

Incest is the sexual contact between family members. It is usually an older brother that takes advantage of the younger sister or brother, one who is more vulnerable. Little did I know how prevalent incest was in the Amish church until I began to work on my own childhood issues. Sometimes people around me started disclosing their childhood stories of incest between family members. I was surprised at the generations of incest.

My childhood seemed like a prison with invisible bars of restraint around me because of the constant need of my brothers. Most of my days were spent outside. I would run and run and scream at the top of my lungs. Deep down I always hoped my brothers would see the error of their ways, but that was a fantasy. I asked myself if the isolation of my true self and feeling alone was really a delusion. Self-rejection felt like a big sister to delusion standing right next to it.

The encouraging parts of the Bible like Hebrews 13:5 is, *"I will never leave thee, nor forsake thee,"* were not real to me. I know that Adam in his aloneness was the one who turned his face from the Father, even though it doesn't' say that Adam experienced incest. When we are alone, I think we turn away from any connection with anyone (even God) to our inner world. God does not usually go where He is not invited, which gives us choice; however, it still allows us to remain alone.

As an adult I have asked myself, how could I have done things differently or reacted differently? Could I have prevented the incest? I don't know. I do know that allowing myself the time and the resources to heal, that rejection had to take a back seat.

In the winter, the sap goes down to the roots of the tree. As the roots grow deeper, it gives the tree stability, and, in the spring, new growth. This phenomenon is at a depth not seen by the eye as the tree struggles for its survival. Similarly, there is little comfort during our growth. I would question if I was on the right track, even though my roots are going deeper.

Give yourself permission to be yourself in every stage of your healing even though you wonder if you are ever going to be normal. I believe you will be in areas that will surprise you later. His eye is on you. The accuser is determined to get your focus on the areas you are lacking. The greater purpose for you is, who God is in you?

I recall one night during a time of desperation, I read that God says in Jeremiah 3:14 that he is married to the backslider. That meant He did not measure my sin and say, "Your sin is so bad that maybe with difficulty I can forgive you." Why do wrong things happen to innocent people? I do not know the answer to that, but I do know that I respect the depth of who God is in me because of my past. I could not have done the changes in me on my own. I believe one of the reasons is that there is reward in life in the struggle for truth.

For me the incest was a few of my older brothers. Thinking back, I questioned if Mom's unhealed wounds of incest blinded her, even though as a parent she was still responsible to protect her children. I couldn't understand why it was so difficult for her not to identify the signs or to be blinded by the indications that signaled misconduct at home? It had to be because she had not dealt with her own issues. As a child, I was convinced that it was my fault, only to learn later that none of it was my fault. I blamed my dad's influence for my brother's indiscretions.

I had to acknowledge that my heart was truly wounded even though I did not want to go through the process of digging down deep into the muck nor expose it all. I tried to push it aside because I did not want to go back to experience the pain for myself or my family. Even my ugly anger I wanted to bury deep by not acknowledging that it was there. Once I acknowledged it, I could then get in touch with the healthy anger at the wrong done to me. My daily optimistic joyful outlook covered my pain.

Satan uses the wounded heart that has not been healed as an open door to come in to wreak havoc. Incest hates exposure. I hated exposure. After the secret is exposed by light, then my pattern of hanging onto the pain can be released.

I have found that Amish and Mennonites live above their pain by not looking at it. We do it very well. Some ignore it, never acknowledging it and unfortunately go to their grave with the pain of their wounds still unaddressed. For years I did the same, however, on my spiritual journey I knew the muck had not all gone. I questioned whether I would ever be free? Susan encouraged me to read specific books on healing. This started my in-depth journey to discover healing.

My decision to do my healing was not encouraged by my new church. There were more important things to do. I had left the Mennonite church before meeting my husband in my midtwenties.

They used the scripture where Jesus confirmed it in Luke 9:62, *"No man having put his hand to the plough, and looking back, is fit for the kingdom of God."* Was I missing something more important to do? Later when I looked at that verse, I realized it meant that if I looked back wishing to return to my old ways, then it would be sin. I would be missing the opportunity to move forward by wanting to return to my past. This allowed me the freedom from the fear of looking back to heal from my experiences.

I began to realize that until I heal and remove the sting of it that it would continue to come up. Satan was there accusing me of being unworthy. Unfit, scarred and dirty he would try to convince me of all those. God had to be bigger. I wanted to not only be free but to know the process to help other victims that were enslaved by what I was exposed to.

Romans 8:32 says, *"He that spared not His own Son, but delivered Him up for us all, how shall He not with Him also freely give us all things."* So was Christ dying on the cross enough to cover all my shortcomings? There is not a thing I could do that would get God to deny the complete work of Jesus in me. If He went to the cross to redeem me including removing the fear of not doing enough good, then He died in vain. Is what He did to free me from the bondage of my tireless work enough or do I somehow need to feel good about myself which negates what Christ did? I had to allow myself to be imperfect.

I was always looking for the healing process to be finished; however, I found healing is done in layers like peeling an onion. One of my layers was that I put a block on my emotions. I pushed my feelings aside. Perhaps that is why I have very few memories of my childhood.

I did not know how to correct it. But I had to consciously determine to not be defensive, by staying open and listening to others before responding. I refused to justify what I did but rather stood back and looked at my rationale as to why I did what I did by discussing it. A good leader is a good listener, who is led by love. When dialogue occurs between two people (such as a husband and wife), the result is they get inspired and motivated to share and change.

BEHIND THE SCENE

Over the years I have gone to a few different therapists. When I would learn of a different way to work on issues, after doing research, I would apply it. One such process I found effective. I would take communion first and ask Jesus to cover me with His blood. The counselor would take me back to a painful memory related to the abuse. Sometimes memories are blocked. For me I got flashbacks of the memory. She would then ask if I saw Jesus in that memory. At first, I did not. I could not understand where God was or why He would allow such a thing. Sometimes I was angry at Him. Let me say here that I believe God in His sovereignty does not intervene in all the wrongs perpetrated on mankind. I learned how important free will is to Him. Without excusing Him, I believe He limits Himself by giving us choices. When I listened and persisted to ask Jesus where He was when it was happening, He responded. I found Christ to be there with me all along. His responses were different with each memory. Once I saw tears running down His face as He watched the injustices. In the process of going through it, much of the pain physically and emotionally was removed. I would suggest you not do this alone at first without someone who is skilled to help you with it.

How does someone get through this? I learned that I had a number of little personalities inside of me. I was surprised to learn how prevalent this phenomenon is. During the act of incest, each little personality would take a turn and come out to handle the abuse. When that little person (girl or boy) would get tired, another would step up to take their turn to handle it. I was unaware of these personalities as well as the memories they kept from me until I went through my healing as an adult. They have since gone to be with Jesus and not integrated into my being. The problem is if they are integrated into your being (as some healing centers advocate), should you be faced with some difficult current event, these personalities can reemerge to help and thwart your own solution to a problem for you as the adult.

There is a thin barrier for me between love and intimacy. The boundaries of what love is was blurred and intimacy is frightening. During the time of my healing, I learned that intimacy was a process of giving slowly in the areas of my relationships that I was not open to before.

If this abuse should be called loving in the home either verbally or sexually, it is confusing to both children and adults. It distorts what is called love, which it is not. In an ideal world, true love does not allow the perpetrator to have his way by either verbally or sexually abusing. The right thing to do as an adult is to resist the attacks of the abuser, all the while encouraging them in the right direction to get help.

The first thing I had to do was to allow myself to grieve. Every detail of the abuse that is ungrieved and unfinished will be acted out in different ways later. Grieve the childhood you never had. Other steps we go through are sadness and anger. My anger was at Mom or Dad for not protecting me, putting the blame on them. Was it not their fault for it happening in the first place? I was incredibly angry with Mom for not protecting me. Dad was never available emotionally nor was he safe.

At times, anxiety came out of nowhere or an overwhelming feeling of guilt originating from past pain. I would be confronted with what seemed to be the same issue that I had just resolved. I refused to push it aside. I'd have to get away to find a safe place to calm down. Emotions can be triggered by a smell, what someone says, or the tone of voice. I wanted to talk to my counselor, but I could not call him as often as I wanted. I felt so out of control. So many negative thoughts came up out of nowhere. I would have repeated dreams of insecurity, especially condemning myself when I was with old friends. I was not as good as them. I would see myself on the outside looking into the circle of friends, wishing I could have true friends inside the circle. Thoughts would come to my mind that things would not get better, and all of this is a trap.

I had to figure out if this battle was a deeper layer of the same issue I had dealt with before that needed more work, or was it because of a pattern of unhealthy thinking that I was accustomed to. Was it the enemy trying to convince me it was still there? Sometimes when I journaled by putting my thoughts on paper, I was able to see more clearly. Some of the other things I did was to call a trusted friend or exercise by walking or bike riding. If I could figure out what triggered me, then I could avoid it or alter my thinking on it as I looked at the trigger.

I would look again at what happened to me. Bizarre as it seems, sometimes it is easier to stay in the same pattern of thinking and acting than to change by going in a different direction. I would look at every detail of behavior that was unfinished and ungrieved and give it to Jesus because it can be acted out again later. It was more difficult for me to forgive what others did to me than for me to confess my own sins and forgive myself. Satan wants to keep you bound in your thinking.

I thought if I can forgive the people who hurt me, then I can just move on. I heard in sermons that "you just have to forgive them." This frustrated me. It is especially easy for Christians to say this when they are uncomfortable with your pain or do not know what to say. Forgiveness is important when various healing processes have been worked on and explored. This is only part of the recovery process. I worked to forgive myself by asking God to fill me with how He thought about me. Today I do not want to allow the failures and mistakes of the past to dictate who I am.

Another layer I went through was being angry. In addition, I felt a deep sadness because of my loss of innocence to be the child I would never experience or know. I was bitter, questioning why I was born into this. Blaming my family would have been easy but resolved nothing. Why do people do the hurtful things they do? Often it is because of the hurtful things that have happened to them.

Sometimes I thought it was because it was my fault; however, I was there as their opportunity.

It had nothing to do with me personally even though it had a huge impact on me personally. Until I can release them, the past pain will not go away.

People who have experienced sexual abuse feel guilty as if they had done something wrong. I would tell God I am sorry, even if it was not my fault. Satan loves to attack and attach himself to my condemnation to destroy my peace because condemnation was my pattern of thinking about myself. When I found nothing to be sorry for, I told Satan to get out. I reminded him that I had repented, and Christ's blood covered me; and that door is not open for him to walk through anymore.

Then it was time for me to forgive. I did not want to give myself permission to do that at first. It felt selfish to take the time; however, I soon realized that whatever time it took to go through the memories and forgive and heal, that it was imperative to allow myself the time and freedom to process it. I had to look at my anger and be allowed to express it by exploring and exploding my reactions without condemnation. Only then was I ready to release my abusers, which freed me from the hold unforgiveness had on me.

Unforgiveness is the responsive feeling of a wrong suffered. It is taking an offense to an area where forgiveness would be good. Forgiveness is under the control of my will; however, if I am unable to be open to the offender as a safe person, then I need to put up boundaries by not allowing them access to reinjure me. Unforgiveness hurts me more than the one who hurt me. Especially if it takes me further to become bitter when I cannot rectify the wrong against me. The memories and emotions were still too raw for me to take the next step. In this process, I found that I needed more time to heal. I do not believe God condemns unforgiveness if my intent was to heal; however, unforgiveness must not allow me to be hateful toward the perpetrator.

Forgiveness has various forms. Each situation is different. Before my dad died, I wrote him a letter. I had grown distant from him. I never liked or agreed with how he treated Mom. He was never available to my siblings or me or aware of what we needed. He exuded his own woundedness. I understood that. He neither have the skill nor did he search or want the knowledge of how to correct it. In my letter, I thanked him for being my dad and stated that I forgive him for not being the dad I needed. At that time, I had still blocked the memory of him abusing me sexually; however, with the new knowledge that I gained of his abuse, I had to forgive again even though he had died. One of the ways my therapist encouraged me to forgive was to write a letter to my abuser, my dad, and how he hurt me. I then forgave him and put a match to it and gave it to God as the smoke ascended. Forgiveness was to free myself.

After going through the stages of healing, it was then time to figure out If I wanted to confront my abusers. I don't believe there is a wrong time or only one right way as to whether I ever confront. Some who choose not to confront find peace by releasing and forgiving. Confronting is a choice. It is important not to feel pressure to do it. It can be done by yourself or with another person or therapist. For me I chose to confront by writing letters. I hoped for an apology. My dad was dead. My brothers were not. My oldest brother apologized over the phone. The next one was living behind a wall too full of shame to address it with me.

When you confront your abuser, there isn't always a good ending. You will not be best friends. That's okay. You may not even like them anymore and want them out of your life. Even if they apologize, some perpetrators should never be trusted, so don't be foolish by inviting them back into the family or left alone with your children, especially when they have not gone through their own healing process. Reconciliation with the perpetrator *is not* required to heal. It is the most difficult. This process is about rebuilding the relationship. It frees the perpetrator.

God understands how we hate the actions of the perpetrator. I would talk to Him about it. I was already living in a different state, which took me out of their environment. I am in contact with them, but to heal does not mean I have to bring them back into my home to be close just because they are my brothers. They themselves have to go through the healing process. In most cases, they also have been abused. That is why abusers abuse others.

It was difficult for me to fathom that Jesus was there the whole time waiting for me to come to Him, especially when at my darkest times, I felt that my life was my greatest loss. It is Him who makes all things possible. He is the one who frees me from the emotions of self-hate, fear, bitterness, disappointment, or the fear of failure. Why do tragic things happen? God desires us to be fully godlike and fully man, all the while teaching us to be whole with His impartation as a human. The great thing about coming out from where you have been is you don't have to walk the same path again. I am a child of the light. Darkness cannot penetrate it. He encourages us to dream. We are His bride. The bride and bridegroom dream of impossibilities.

Christ, with every lash of the whip, was able to forgive His abusers during His time of greatest need. Put your judgmental list away, and bloom in who God has made you. God will give you a new heart and spirit. When I am delivered and free from my critical eye, I will see them as God sees them. God's spirit always works in them for every problem. I refuse to judge them where they are. I do not know what they have gone through to get them to the place they are at. Who knows why anyone does anything they do? What if they are put there for me to learn not to be judgmental?

No one can tell you how to do your healing. That is your own personal unique journey, and everyone is different. Should a compulsion to repeat the abuse that you encountered as a child come to the front, no matter how bizarre it is, look again at what happened to you. Look at every detail that is unfinished and ungrieved without fear of rejection, and seek help. Since completing therapy some years ago, I continue to heal when any unhealed emotional memories come up. I trust Jesus for His thorough work, and sometimes I schedule an appointment for a follow-up with my therapist when I have questions or need to resolve an issue.

Today I am more aware of the signs of abuse in others. It is my prayer that I can help guide the person in the right direction, who may be ready to process their healing. God is our restorer.

CHAPTER 15

Recently I was called back to the bedside of my youngest brother, who is just a year older than me, who was dying. I looked at my two older brothers who were also visiting and realized that my feelings of dislike for them were very much alive. I thought I had forgiven them. Through the years, I had visited their families for just a few hours, but this was different. Those were short visits. This time, at my brother's bedside, it was days of talking and interacting.

Not only did I have to face my younger brother dying but also my two oldest brothers who were leaning on me for emotional support. I assisted them with their routine of taking medications and getting around physically. I found a lack of love and compassion inside me. I cried out to God to help me because I simply did not have it in me. I knew my attitude had to change. One of them had apologized years ago; and the other, with stooped shoulders, carried too much shame to apologize.

Then the answer came. I knew they hated what they had done to me. I saw the shame and the prison they were still in as they related to me. It was up to me to free them from their prison. I remembered when Jesus said in John 2:23, "*Whose soever sins you remit, [forgive] they are remitted [forgiven] unto them, and whose soever sins ye retain they are retained.*" That verse made sense to me for the first time. I could forgive myself for my reaction and be loving.

This was not the time to discuss the past by bringing it to their attention, but as difficult as this time was for me, I would take the opportunity to respond to them in a loving way, which to me was what I believe Christ would have done. If I wrote my thoughts on paper, they would have gone something like this. "Concerning what you did to me sexually as a child, I know you are ashamed of what you did. It is written all over you. Because this is too difficult for you to talk about, today I free you from the shame and the satanic hold it has on you."

The following year, my oldest brother, Mose, was dying. Before he died, he called me one day to ask if Joe had ever apologized for doing what he did to me sexually as a child. I responded that he had not. In the plans for the funeral, I asked my brother Joe why he would not consider going to the funeral. I knew he had an excuse of being feeble. He responded that he could not be a part of the family even though he and Mose had always been close. Something was not right. Some months later, when I called to check up on him, I began questioning him at length as to why he did not feel that he could be a part of the family. He said, "I do not know why I did what I did growing up."

I then put it all together. Before he died, Mose had confronted him concerning what he did to his sisters and asked him to make it right. Shame now kept Joe from feeling worthy of being a part of the family. How could he approach what could possibly mean rejection from me? He went on to say that he was the worst. "Mom even took me to see a counselor," he said. "It did not help." I then realized Mom did more to stop what she thought was happening to my little sister only.

By this time, he was sobbing, hardly able to speak, saying, "I'm sorry, I am so sorry." I was able to tell him that I forgave him. I felt only pity and love for him. His childhood had been very difficult. I repeatedly said that it was important for him to forgive himself. He finally understood it. He said he had talked to his pastor who also said he must forgive himself. At the end of the conversation, we both experienced a peace that was very real.

CHAPTER 16

Growing up in a family of dysfunction, I built a house of false fear to protect my dark secrets. I had to build a cover to protect my inner world. It must never come down nor would I allow anyone in. I was convinced I would be rejected if I did. No one would like me. To keep everyone out, I had to keep my walls high. There is no interaction or light inside. I started to agree with what Satan said about me. The "I am nots" stack up: I am not smart enough. I am not good enough. I will never measure up. No one can come into my secret space. To face alienation would be terrifying. Or if anyone showed affection, I would allow them in only so far.

What I learned as a child was to function outside of that inside world. I would follow the rules of the church and their expectations. It got me approval, affection, and safety. Following the rules protected me. Walking with God was my number one ambition and a covering around me to protect me. I kept busy by focusing on being a mom, keeping up the home, working and counseling others with my husband as a pastor's wife. My inside world of self-value was still flawed. I did not understand the importance of allowing God in to heal me completely. I did talk to Him, but my flawed beliefs about myself were still there. I needed to take the next step with counseling. My survival depended on it.

If this happened to you when you were a child, your dark past will most likely surface, affecting your future until you allow the healing process to take place. I pray you experience God's love in this. Kindness shattered my walls, but it took time. I could not put a limit on it. Everyone is not the same. Jesus is the healer who comes to heal those deep wounds that come up in memories and dreams.

When I was taking a class on inner healing, the instructor taught about narcissism. It was a new concept for me, but one that I believe belongs here as it touches on why some people are occupied with themselves by drawing attention to themselves in unhealthy ways. Narcissism may be rooted in repeated negative corrections and lack of encouragement from the parents. Or perhaps they cannot get their needs met because there are other siblings to care for, demanding the parents' attention. Instead of neglect, they need to be hugged and told they are loved even when being instructed. Busy parents have difficulty finding a way to encourage their children by helping them to shine by going in the direction they are designed to go. Sometimes I have noticed when a child is caught in a wrong action, the punishment in that wrong is enough to correct the child without further punishment from a parent.

If the child is inclined toward narcissistic behavior, the child builds what is called a house of cards. These cards put next to each other can be as elaborate as a two-to-three-story house stacked on top of each other. Building that house of cards is what happens as they start to build their own inside world where they fantasize about their worth. They are always looking for approval by adding another card to build themselves up. When approval and value are missing, their inner world is shattered, and their weak house of cards falls. Their house of cards is so fragile that it can be destroyed by simply blowing on it.

As an adult, when that child looks into a pool of water (or a mirror), they would be admiring themselves. Why? Because in their world, where no one else is approving of them, they turn inward, satisfying their needs with admiration for themselves. In their family or church, they could be seen as prideful, self-centered, or boastful. This state is delicate, sensitive, and easily misunderstood.

If you were to confront the adult narcissist, who is convinced of the correctness of their viewpoint, they will strongly defend it. It results in defending their perspective as they see it. No one can come into that fragile house of cards. This is to protect their image. They will make you feel like it is your fault for not agreeing with them. Adults who have to control or need things to be perfect cannot allow you into their inner house of cards. As for me, I refuse to make my truth, which is my perspective, an idol or a force that others must bow to as a standard of truth. If discussion is allowed, they will find their way.

If only we as parents could find a way to love with kindness instead of criticizing, to touch the heart of the child, they would believe they are worthy. Why not find ways to encourage the child, especially when it is difficult for the child to follow your rules. *"A soft answer turns away wrath; but grievous words stir up anger,"* Proverbs.15:1 says.

A functional family strives to meet the needs of their children. In a dysfunctional family, the child meets the needs of the parents.

Every problem has a promise. We are never the victim of impossibilities. Never do we exhaust His grace. Christ in us makes problems into possibilities. He desires for us to value Him. He loves you because He is love, even in your darkest time. He frees you from the low self-esteem and rejection that the enemy would love for you to feel and be bound by. David had seven hundred wives, and he premeditated murder, yet he was a man after God's heart. God loves me more than my sin or the rules.

The times that I believe I needed to look back was to break the cycle of pain that sin was able to put on me and attaching its tentacles to bring me down, especially when times get tough and the enemy whispers that I am not worth it. Those tentacles must be broken. The children of Israel wanted to go back to Egypt after God had delivered them out of it, which is why they were not fit to enter the promised land. It is common to want to go back to one's former state. I do not want to go back to living in what I grew up in but to learn from it and to move forward to heal and become an overcomer and live out God's purpose for me.

Now I know that not all Amish families have these issues of incest, but far too many do. They are good people. So why are so many afraid to talk about what is happening to their children? The secrets of your generations are bound to repeat themselves if they are not looked at and talked about in an environment of safety for both the abused and the abuser.

I'm not talking about going up in front of the church to confess to the whole congregation. That would heap shame on their heads. It is important for the survivor to have a safe place to be able to talk without the perpetrator or parents attending unless the survivor wants the parents there. The child needs an environment to be able to share freely. The desired result is to get healing and understanding despite what happened to them. It must be without shame or blame.

This goes for the perpetrator as well. My normal response might be to come down hard on the one that took advantage of the younger, more vulnerable sibling. I wonder in the dysfunctional family what the reason is when the older ones are out of control sexually toward the younger ones. Perhaps they also were abused by another person or older member of the family.

Watching TV one day, I was flipping through the channels. I ran across a live court trial, which caught my attention. It was about two Amish brothers that were brought up on charges of incest to their younger sister. The presentation went on to say that when she got older, she worked for the family's "English" neighbors. Eventually she disclosed to the neighbors what was happening at home with her brothers. The story did not show the process, but my guess is she went to the law with the help of her English neighbors when her home situation did not change. The older brother went to prison, whereas the other was a juvenile, which got him probation.

I was amazed as I watched the children's parents and Amish friends file into the courtroom supporting the brothers who shamed their daughter, for bringing such an action against them legally. The girl's dress told me that she had left the Amish church. My heart was so sad as she seemed so hurt and disillusioned by her family turning against her. Seeking help outside the Amish church seemed her only defense against the wrong that was perpetrated on her.

How could this have been handled differently? No one was there to help the family navigate through this painful ordeal. To me there was no support system in place to help with what happens so often in a closed group of people. When the survivor tries to expose it, there can be so much grief and misunderstanding for the survivor and the perpetrators. The desire by the adults surrounding it is to sweep it under the carpet. It is so sad. Painful as it is, it must be brought out from hiding to an open discussion among knowledgeable adults—adults whom they can trust to meet with each separately without pressure from parents to attend the sessions. It must be an environment of safety for the survivor to be able to talk freely. This is a process that requires more than one meeting to repair. This often requires help from a professional counselor. Because the survivor has been so subjected to this pattern, it is important to not shame or place guilt on the survivor for taking time to heal.

What I know now about then

In our cells is the blueprint that programs us. Our physical appearances are what we get from our ancestor's DNA, which are handed down to our children from generation to generation. There is still a part of the DNA code that puzzles scientists. They have not been able to map a certain portion of it. I question if this could possibly be the patterns of behavior including our strengths and weaknesses. Could this be what is meant when it talks about the sins of the fathers being visited onto the fourth generation in the Bible? Our genetic code goes back to even further than our parents, and some have suggested that it goes all the way back to Adam.

In counseling, I learned that the predisposition my family had to sexual improprieties could be a pattern of sin in my genetic makeup. Mom told me once that she was disclosing to the pastor's wife about some of the sexual sins of Dad and Grandpa's past, and she said, "Well, that is just the way that side of the family is." Mom was not happy with that conclusion.

So when the temptation comes, would my family be more susceptible to sexual misconduct? If this is not addressed or covered over, does that open the door for the cycle to be repeated? I believe Satan takes advantage through those kinds of open doors, and if those doors are not closed by repenting for my generational sins, then it can pass on to the next generation.

The plan of God is for all to be overcomers. In counseling, I asked Jesus to come into the areas of those painful memories to close all the open doors to my responses of self-hate, blame, shame, and to dress my wounds by cleaning them with His blood.

Forgiveness is not for what was done to me but for the destructive patterns it created in me. If I continue to be plagued by shame, self-hate, and self-blame, then I need to look deeper by forgiving myself. I repent of what was foisted on me by the abuse, allowing Satan access to destroy my life, even if the abuse was not my fault. I ask Jesus for a clean garment. His desire is for me. It is important to walk in what He saw for me because He said I was chosen before the foundation of the world.

Important lessons learned

Control. Control is the power to direct or to determine the behavior of another. I don't think we would consider ourselves as a god, but setting ourselves above another, or judging as a god, is control. This is the door to personal idolatry.

If you are controlling, you are a god of your world, which makes your life like a pressure cooker ready to explode by insisting to get it right. Things must be in order, which makes it impossible for the ones around you to get it right. There is no freedom in diversity of thought because the controller has put you in a box to think their way. The controller then assumes the responsibility of the decisions for the family.

A controller takes the place of the Lordship of Jesus Christ over the controlled one. This makes it impossible for them to see God's grace for themselves or see it for the other person. Unfortunately, this blocks the grace that would enable them to make the changes needed for the relationship, resulting in a recurring failure and heartache. After the controller looks at the devastation from his uncontrolled rage on his family, he fails to see where he needs to change. Instead, he insists that his family do as he says. When this does not happen, they make new judgments as to why. These criticisms bring more dysfunction and sadness when their rules cannot be followed perfectly enough. This further isolates the controller. They believe that they do not love them. The lack of concern or submission by the one being controlled is seen as evidence that they are not loved. As the controller sits on his throne of judgment the nonsubmissive one has their own belief of what is right. In the end, the closeness, which was meant to be, is destroyed.

Interestingly, I attract controllers in my relationships. I was brought up in a church with many rules and have gravitated to controlling churches as an adult. It is what I have been used to. I have more to say on this subject here because being controlled has been at the front of my struggles. Its existence snuck in to blind me, and unknowingly I would get enmeshed into a situation before I realized that I needed to find my way out of it. True submission is important; however, those who wish to be in control may act as the authority but in fact are controllers. My submission is yielding my will to God first, not to the controller. Now when my gut says there is something that stinks here, I can say no.

My experience sometimes made me feel that men are harsh and authoritarian, accepting me only when I do as they require with no consideration of my opinion or ideas. Only when I agree and give in am I accepted. When I allow my will or opinion to be silenced against my better knowledge, because I know his issues from his early childhood wounding are acting out as he expresses his need to have it his way, then this is a wide-open door for him to continue to abuse on an emotional, spiritual, or physical level. I believe it is here with my own discomfort in confronting that I must say, "This is the way I see it." If I don't stand up for my opinion, it will make me angry the more I think about it later. The root of this comes from the lack of assurance from a trustworthy father that my opinion matters.

A controller has to be in control verbally and can be physically aggressive toward a person. Frequently they need to be admired for their point of view. The desire for power silences all in its path. They easily shift the blame onto others, even shaming the one who does not share their way of thinking. It is usually the male figure in the home whose attitude toward his wife or children is one of disapproval. It is humiliating to all within earshot of the turmoil as there is no restraint when the explosive outbursts happen. The controller is justified because he believes his perception is right in how he perceives he was wronged. This does not allow for any open discussion. With time, the once close relationships become tarnished, destroying the family unit by isolating all. With shoulders stooped, the rights of each person are nonexistent. With no open discussion allowed, there is no process to resolve the problem. There is no safety in trusting him.

Controllers push people away and create a shell around everyone involved, isolating all and making it impossible to have a close intimate relationship. Sex for the spouse becomes a duty. The family walks on eggshells, waiting for what might trigger the next outburst. This kills respect from the children toward their dad. In a twisted way, the children lose respect toward the abused mother as well for not standing up for herself in the dispute. They can become verbally abusive toward Mom, believing it is okay to yell at her. The girls can learn to take a subservient role or become angry without knowing why. They justify it because they see it as being normal. Or sometimes they feel sorry for the wounded one, which further confuses what is right.

Sometimes controllers get energized by lecturing, demanding respect. Their sharp critical observation of a situation is seen by them as constructive criticism. Often, they become disillusioned with people criticizing them, which makes them even more harsh. There is no negotiation while they announce proudly that they are the authority. In the animal kingdom, the male species takes the initiative to dominate the female. This is what is known as the alpha male. For humans, this is not our model.

Deep down, the controller fights insecurity. Loneliness and isolation are their companions. Telling themselves they are right, with an air of superiority, they often refuse outside help from a pastor or counselor.

My early training taught obedience. In the church, I don't ever recall experiencing that who I was as a person was important to the few spiritual leaders that held control over me. The rules were read to the congregation twice a year before communion and foot washing. Questions of curiosity were allowed privately, but no opposition or disagreements to the rules. This subservient programming got me in trouble later in life. When I followed leaders, whom I learned later were seeking their own validation, I came under their control by following their leadership. As a giver, it was satisfying and gave me purpose. I knew that I was needed. I worked to please. With time, I lost my ability to disagree and separate myself from his opinions. I lost my leverage to disagree. It is a seductive manipulation, which means my worth is only considered when my subservience is to obey. This gives the controller power over me.

The end result of feeling like my way of thinking or doing things was wrong, was shame. Eventually I became "a nothing." It affirmed what I was most afraid of—that I did not matter. My obedience to authority was flawed. I was flawed. I was controlled based on mistrust of my own opinions and insecurity. My foundation fell with no footing. Insecurity, fear, and self-hatred was hitting at my core. Am I a big nothing? Is shame intended to silence me, making me feel alone? The controller continues by disrespecting me, thereby finding power in doing so.

When our reality and attitudes are based on the teachings of other people, and our decisions are made because of someone else's decisions, especially against our own inner beliefs we are being controlled. This makes it impossible for Jesus to be the reality He wants to be in my life because the other person is taking that position. Today much of religion is about performance and control. Is that why I am comfortable and attracted to controlling people, because that is what I was trained in?

Jesus walked in love, and yet He never allowed anyone to take advantage of Him. Love does not seek to be validated by someone else's judgments. The law imposed control over people. It never changed a heart. Today we can change because we have one God, Jesus, and the Holy Spirit with love at the core.

At times I would stay in my own world wondering whether to continue to tolerate this constant critique. This dysfunction of disagreement and control for me was not true submission. True submission is a joy to be in partnership finding ways to contribute, to be something they would have a difficult time doing on their own by accomplishing it together. Otherwise, you're walking on eggshells wondering when the next explosion will occur. Even in your interactions with other people they, can become jealous, which sets them off. This could make one wonder, thinking, "Oh he really loves me, wanting me for himself." Don't be fooled. This is not true love.

When someone disrespects you in a conversation, this is a clue that I have found effective. Ask them to explain by repeating the comment back to you because you don't understand. Many times, they change the comment as they have time to think about what they said. Don't accept a put-down as a rejection because it can haunt you until you hate yourself. Do not allow anyone to steal who you are.

In my experience, sometimes when I shared my thoughts with my husband, I learned that most of the time, he took an opposite point of view than mine. As my opinion was invalidated routinely, insecurity and lack of confidence demolished what I thought I knew or could express. One time I wondered what would happen if I presented the opposite conclusion than what I believed on a subject. As he proceeded to disagree with me, he took my original point of view. When I told him what I had done, I suggested that it was one way we could agree. He didn't see it that way and became angry with me.

Addressing by talking about their behavior after the blowup is the only remedy I know for this besides counseling. One evening at church, a man of God pulled me to the side and said, "God is teaching you how to fight." He knew that I knew what he was talking about. I was upset, thinking that I knew how to stand up for myself and fight, but reflecting back, I didn't have a clue. Today when an issue begins to escalate, I excuse myself and go to another room. My response is, "You are obviously angry. When you want to talk about it without the accusatory rage, then I am open to listening."

Sometimes when leaving the verbal interaction, it can anger them more because they are trying to get their point across, and now they just lost their audience. This can ramp up the abuse from verbal to physical by grabbing and possibly hitting. This has not happened to me; however, if they do become violent, then it is extremely important for you to escape or develop an exit strategy.

When reason finally has the upper hand following an angry outburst, they frequently say, "I'm sorry." With time, that phrase loses its meaning. One would wonder if they were truly sorry because I know it will probably happen again. It was not because of my problem. It was because they have an anger problem. How long do I take it? Am I okay with being beat down to where my opinion does not matter? My submission is to the Lord first. When I know who Christ is in me, only then can I submit to my husband because it is the Lord in him that I submit to, not to his anger because he said so.

When things cool down, ask the Lord to show you how He thinks about it. When you have it, approach him in hopes of a discussion. Usually by that time, they know they were the one out of control. If he does not want to look at it, I will continue to bring him back to the incident and look at what angered him. Sometimes I say, "Your facts may be correct, but the way you delivered it was wrong, which makes it wrong." For me, as with most women, I like to resolve it by discussing every aspect, which is called full circle. Men want to forget it, let it go by not discussing it, thinking that with time, it will all be okay. It is not okay! I have learned how to confront, and I am still learning. It is not pleasant, but it is part of his and my salvation and my learning not to be passive. If I feel controlled and shut down by saying yes without question to his demands or way of thinking, then there is no freedom.

There is a medical term called Attention Deficit Hyperactive Disorder (ADHD) that is found more often in males that have quick outbursts. These people have a difficult time with the normal response time that it takes for a normal brain to react to a problem. Once they are triggered, they quickly react. There are a number of theories about this. Some say as a child they have not learned delayed gratification skills by processing how to solve a problem. A trigger, which activates a problem, then takes them to an immediate reaction with no reasoning before reacting. They want immediate results. A trigger can take them from A to Z without processing any of the steps to problem solve that go-between.

The barometer for me is this: Are they willing to look at the issue and work to change it? If his answer is, "That is just the way I think," that is not an excuse. If they choose not to change, there is nothing one can do because it is their choice, not yours. Friends and family are helpless to intervene in this situation. It is challenging for the victim when they have been put down for years, often being called stupid, unworthy, or the one at fault. They find it impossible to think of branching out, moving forward to do it alone by being independent. It is important to find a way to protect yourself and your children. The choice is tough, but the right choice is to ask for help. This is where friends and local agencies can help you. If my personal responsibility requires change to guard and protect my heart and my children, then I will work on that to honor it.

One of the stages after a blowup is that the abuser becomes sweet and apologetic. This is what is known as the "honeymoon stage." The abuser does sweet things to make up for what they did or said. The recipient of the abuse then lets down their guard, working to forgive until it happens again when she or he does something the other dislikes.

I am reminded of a poem called "Managing from the Heart" by Hyler Bracey, Jack Rosenblulm, Aubrey Sanford, and Roy Trueblood.

> Hear and understand me.
> Even if you disagree, please don't make me wrong.
> Acknowledge the greatness within me. Remember
>   to look for my loving intentions.
> Tell me the truth with compassion.

"*Now this is eternal life: that they know you, the only true God, and Jesus Christ, whom you have sent,*" (John 17:3 KJV). The word *know* in that verse is intimacy. As we experience Him then, we can then truly know who we are. He is love.

Love does not seek its own. It takes no account or record of a wrong suffered. When Christ's love is my first desire and intention, then I can trust in the process of what's in front of me. That may sound arrogant, but it is not. If I have other intentions as trying to fix someone, then the danger is that my motive could be centered on meeting my own need to feel good about myself. The result will be trying to remove the speck out of the other's eye when I have a plank in mine.

Sometimes a spouse can demand that you love them because they think they deserve it. Real love does not insist on that. It took me some time to identify healthy love when I started healing. Accepting the reality of what I suffered in the abuse does not define who I am. If it did, that would imprison me, and that is a farce. God does not waste my suffering.

If I look at the world and judge everything in the light of my past pain, then this cycle could cause me endless pain. As overcomers, there is no avoiding the pain, but to know as we heal and become healed, we can help others. We leave no one behind nor allow anyone to suffer alone. This is the lens of love that we look through that takes us to a brighter world.

Love is there to listen to the other person without taking personal offense even if their complaint was about us, nor is it trying to persuade them to our point of view. It is their journey, and they are processing what they did right or wrong without my interpretation. Love points them to the master of love without condemnation. Trust is to know that Christ will encourage and lead them into all truth.

My husband and I were pastors for a season, and we would counsel people in the church. One of the challenges that we faced was having people put us on a pedestal by looking up to us, thinking that we had some special spiritual knowledge. People and leaders can get bloated from this kind of adulation. This created a wall between them and us. It is a challenge to take down those walls when peoples' guards had been up for so long. Feeling defensive fueled their feelings of guilt, rejection, shame, or abandonment.

If my husband or I would have come on strong by correcting the person being counseled by the rules of what we believed, it would further isolate them. Sometimes in their previous counseling sessions, they had been criticized by other pastors, which made them defensive. Instead, when we worked through it with them, without condemnation, they would be able to process their needs by opening up to talk about what happened to them. I found it important to sit with them, encouraging them, giving hope and grace with no condemnation. It is important to find someone who can help you heal through the difficulties and feel safe by not sharing details with another.

Legalism. Legalism is defined as the excessive adherence to the law. It is a set of laws or rules that focuses on performance to follow those rules perfectly. What is following the law excessively or what is just right? What if I do it wrong? Have I followed the commandments of the Bible or worked enough to get me to the goal of going to heaven? If all I need to do is believe what is right, is that enough to save me? Have I said the right prayer or prayed long enough? Or will my mind continue to torment me as I wonder, fearing that I am missing out spiritually? I wonder if my performance with all my limitations of achievements is enough. This thinking separates me further from God. Even the finality of death can be a fearful thing, which further isolates me from God. This cycle makes me more of a slave to work harder to do it perfectly.

Legalism is control from the outside in. Was God disappointed with me? That would haunt me. Do I have to put up a façade to be spiritual? Does God love me for who I am? Self-discipline is structure from the outside in. Self-control is from the inside out. Does spiritual growth develop maturity by some organization passing a law? In Colossians 2:14, it says, *"Blotting out the handwriting of ordinances that was against us, which was contrary to us, and took it out of the way, nailing it to the cross."*

In the world, a nation operates by a set of laws. Those laws are backed up by an authority. In the United States, we have three divisions of power backed up by a legal document called the Constitution. Judges have authority to implement the laws. Police execute power backed by those laws, which oversees people to make sure those laws are followed.

In the Old Testament times, there were over six hundred laws that the Jews were living by. There was an occasional visitation from God. During the time of Christ, the Pharisees were more than just legalists following the law exactly. They were externalists. An externalist is one who depends on the outward appearance to show acts of obedience. They had such a difficult time receiving the words and examples of Jesus because they were followers of the law. In the Bible, the Jews took the system of the law that should have served the people and instead made the people to serve the system. They missed love as being the motivating factor.

They reduced what should have been a relational walk with God to an outward observation, all of which had little or no value regarding the motive of the heart. Matthew 15:8–9 says, *"This people draweth nigh unto me with their mouth, and honoreth me with their lips, but their hearts are far from me. But in vain they do worship me; teaching for doctrines the commandments of men."*

In the New Testament, it changed. Christ gave two commandments in Mark 12:29–31.

> *And Jesus answered him, "The first of all commandments is, 'Hear, O Israel: The Lord our God is one Lord: And thou shalt love the Lord thy God with all thy heart, and with all thy soul, and with all thy mind, and with all thy strength: This is the first commandment. And the second is like this, thou shalt love thy neighbor as thyself. There is none other commandment greater than these.'"*

This is true authority in God's kingdom.

Christ's authority was shown when He chose to wash the disciple's feet, thereby, honoring them. The ego was put aside. In a relationship, I believe that true spiritual authority will reproduce Christ in another with God indwelling as the authority. For me this passion for this law of love is love, joy, peace, and longsuffering because God is love.

First John 4:8 says, *"He that loveth not knoweth not God; for God is love."* Romans 13:10 says, *"Love worketh no ill to his neighbor: therefore love is the fulfillment of the law."* The law imposed control over the people. It did not change a heart or make anyone whole or free. If the law would have done all these things, it should have made people from long ago righteous, which means Jesus would not have needed to come.

Outward judgment based on rules is characteristic of an externalist. Externalists do not experience the peace of knowing God's love and acceptance because they do not look inward by listening to what the Holy Spirit is saying in their heart. When there is no intimacy with God, He cannot direct from our hearts. When intimacy is replaced by the rules, a false sense of security happens. This then is followed by finding fault in others and thereby elevating themselves. They measure godliness externally by constantly comparing and condemning. With the externalist, God is not followed from the heart. Behavior is most important to the externalist.

One of the downfalls I have encountered in church leadership is when the leader scrutinizes another church's doctrine or their behavior. This takes the spotlight off the leader and gives them more control. In the eyes of the people, they see the leader as an authority. In addition, it offsets the criticism that would be against themselves. It can create fear and self-doubt in the followers. As a result, the leader does not have to deal with their own issues. This is religion parading as a ministry, telling others how they must live.

Our minds are good at analyzing and reasoning. Religion, unlike God, speaks to my head, whereas God always speaks to my heart. When my mind has questions, I then ask Jesus and the Holy Spirit for answers. I leave it to Him and trust Him for answers. I am encouraged when I read the journey of the patriarchs in the Word. He is not the author of confusion, condemnation, or a fear that I am missing something.

Religion gave me safety by operating under the control of the leaders; however, it really put me in a straitjacket with little room for a different point of view. This took away my freedom to question. When a leader presented the rules of the organization, which have been passed down for generations, I found it difficult to challenge him with a different way of looking at it. Yes, I was timid, but I also realized the leader believed he had the final answer with his interpretation of the Bible as it pertained to the rules. This made it impossible for change to occur because change is feared in the church. If you have a different insight or idea about the subject, you are often looked upon as being rebellious. Acceptance from the group then becomes conditional when you don't meet the standard of their thinking. Love is then withheld, along with scrutiny, which makes it conditional. You are then controlled by fear.

After I left the Mennonite church, I would interpret the Bible as I had been taught for many years. It was very difficult for me to read the Bible differently. I saw all the rules of the "do nots." The programmed voice in my head reminded me of the rules followed by criticism and condemnation rather than love with freedom and joy. I began to get insight into the meaning of the scriptures in the context to the Hebrew culture and language at the time when it was written. I am still learning. The Bible was written by more than forty authors in different historical periods, yet God inspired each one of them. Every time I ask God to give me a hunger to know more of Him, He does.

Grace. Grace is the empowering presence of God, so when He looks at me, He sees His essence. God accepts me as I am. Grace to me is where I could never accomplish being good enough. It is Him coming and making it not what I deserve but giving me love and acceptance. I give thanks for this.

Loving and celebrating who God made me gives my life purpose. He keeps no record of a wrong or the list that you are afraid He will read. You can't see the person you are meant to be when you cling to rules that humans have proven they cannot live up to. This causes one to distort who God is by believing He is strict, angry, austere, or wanting justice. It is interesting to note that religion calls you a sinner. Jesus calls you a saint. *"I do not frustrate the grace of God, for if righteousness comes through the law then Christ died in vain"* (Galatians 2:21 KJV).

Identity. When He wants to share His thoughts with me, I often find it comes to me as a different thought than I would ordinarily have. It is a time of "Ahh, that makes sense!" Trust it. He is talking to you. Stop doubting it or confessing that He couldn't be talking to you. Hold the thought, write it down, and ask Him to confirm it.

Romans 8:29–30 says, *"For whom He did foreknow, He also did predestinate to be conformed to the image of his Son, that he might be the firstborn among many brethren. Moreover, whom he did predestinate, them he also called: and whom he called, them he also justified: and whom he justified, them he also glorified."* This He did before we were born. Some translations have used the word *predestined*, but that would take it to the future tense, and the original text does not have a future tense. Isaiah 40:5 says, *"And now, saith the Lord that formed me from the womb."* He has known us for a long time because we were already in His belly.

Self-esteem. To me self-esteem is the subjective evaluation of my own worth and beliefs about myself. It comes from being accepted for being me, which comes from being loved as a child. Low self-esteem, however, is the mind's critical evaluation that evaluates every situation encountered.

During the times when I faced depression, which is a sign of low self-esteem, my mind would fluctuate between telling myself that I was a good person and telling myself that deep down I was not. I would look at all the areas where I worked to excel by having the right kind of reactions. But deep down inside, there was a small seed of knowing that I was bad. This black dot made me work to be perfect on the outside. If I kept doing the right thing, would it make up for how hollow and awful a person I was on the inside?

Women I believe face self-esteem issues because they have been devalued throughout history. The struggle of self-doubt and inadequacy with women of abuse are flawed at a core level. When a child is denied the reassurance that they are good and the expression of love is denied, their worth is in question. There is an underlying nagging shame that eats away at one's self-worth. It alienates and isolates. In order to cover this nothingness, work then becomes the important fix to hide one's unworthiness. During the times when they felt good about themselves, the negative feelings under the surface would come up when they faced a conflict. They lose the good things about who they are, and in a moment, they easily trash themselves so effectively that the abuser doesn't even have to be there to convince them that they have no value or will ever have any impact in the world.

Struggling through the ups and downs of all the bottled-up negative self-hate emotions from the memories, I had to give myself permission to feel it all by talking about it and reprograming myself to love and value myself. With time, this negative self-talk becomes less frequent. This is why I choose to be a survivor and not a victim. Staying in the victim mode gives one an excuse to be sorry for themselves because of the many old injustices plus looking for any new ones that may happen.

"As Christ is, so are we." He is the only one that can truly assure me that who I am is important. I trust that when I invite God into all the areas of my pain that I am a child of the King. I want Him to love me for who I am and not for what I can do for Him.

While growing up and before going through my healing, my perceptions in conversations or situations were twisted and frequently unfounded. In a group of people, I heard what other people did not hear in the conversations. People were unaware of my insecurities and feelings of inferiority. I was convinced they were probably disapproving of me. When I asked them to clarify my perceptions of a conversation we had among ourselves, they were surprised and affirmed that my thinking was not true.

My low self-esteem would bring up the feeling that there must be something wrong with me. Then I would trash talk myself for bringing up the subject. On the other hand, if in my shyness I did not attempt to clarify what happened, it opened the door for it to seem real, regardless of the truth of what happened. This caused me to judge other people, and often I assumed other people were better than me, which made me feel even worse about myself. Then my inner dialogue would start by me trashing myself saying things like, "That was really dumb of you."

The Bible says not to think of yourself more highly than you ought to, but it does not give any guidelines as to what is too much. In my church and family, any word starting with *self* was questionably wrong because it pointed to oneself. The only good self-word that I can recall was *selfless*. My understanding of what that meant was to give until one experience's fatigue, then continuing to give more, even if it depletes all your energy. However, in defense of those times, on workdays it felt good to work beyond one's perceived limits. At the end of the projects, there was satisfaction in the accomplishments; and relationships happened, which also builds self-worth.

When self-esteem is low, it takes risk to move beyond what I am comfortable with, to look for a relationship, which is known to build self-esteem. In taking that risk, it is important to know that rejection is a possibility. I would tell myself that I was okay before I tried to pursue a friendship, and if I was rejected, I was still okay. I did not lose anything that was not there to begin with.

If rejected, it is important to control any negative self-talk like, "I will never have good friends." Self-doubt is already in existence, and people can make you feel bad; however, in reality, people do not make you feel anything. It is your reaction and response. I had to be okay with being uncomfortable. Risk equals growth. I will take a deep breath and try again.

A few guidelines for healthy relationships that I found are, they give positive feedback and allow you to share ideas and thoughts that give insight. They give support without criticism when you express your ideas or express the goals for your life? Before I talk to potential friends, I tell myself, "I can do this. I am valuable as a friend. I am worthy to be loved."

Human touch is another way to boost self-esteem. If this makes you feel afraid, believe and know that you are valuable as a friend. I need at least four hugs a day.

Pride. Pride or boasting was feared growing up and in the old-order Amish church because the Bible talks about the haughty and prideful. If you are grateful for what God has done in your life, that is not pride. That is celebrating who Jesus is in you.

Jesus said not to think of yourself more highly than you ought to, but He did not say what is too much. Is your joy and love in your relationship with Him pride? I think not. If anything, I see that pride grows when we put ourselves down, thinking it is humility. I recall asking one of the older women in the church to teach my Sunday school class because I was going to be away the following Sunday. She said, "Oh no, I don't think I can do that." She questioned whether she was qualified. This was common, and I did not feel it was my place to reassure her that she is spiritual enough to teach a second grade Sunday school class. My response was not good looking back as I, too, was judgmental. I said, "If you don't think you can, then you can't," which surprised her. It felt like she wanted me to assure her that she could do it, which I could have, but I felt like it was pride in what passed as humility in her inability—pride in doing menial, nonimportant tasks, which paraded as humility.

Envy. Envy is rooted in how we think about ourselves. It causes one to look from the left to the right instead of upward and into the heart. Its harmful aspects are easy to hide and difficult to admit. In the story of Joseph, I wonder if the brothers didn't believe that they would no longer have to listen to his boasting about his grandiose dreams, plus they would get more love from their father. The lie is that if one implements or does harm, then they will likely get what they want.

It is a dark side of us that secretly celebrates when someone who has more and seems to have it all together suffers of falls. Envy is not how much one has because if what one has is not enough, then what you envy would still not be enough even after you have it.

What breaks the cycle of envy? Gratitude! Yes, gratitude even in the little things.

Fear. Love destroys unhealthy fear. Healthy fear is my protection. It can be a result of a new direction or an opportunity that opens for a change like a different job or getting married. God limits what He could be to me by giving me choice. He is so committed that He went to the cross submitting to my darkness. This pushes me to pray, asking for wise decisions.

Unhealthy fear is the fear of what people think. It controls and asks, "What if." Fear and manipulation go together and are what perpetrators use to seduce their victims.

When I became a young adult and older, obedience to the rules of the church was expected. These rules as interpreted by leadership from the Bible was expected. It was implied that my disobedience would cause me to go to hell unless I repented. If I obeyed, I could hope to go to heaven unless there was something God found wrong with me on judgment day. Now that to me was fear! But my mind would wander to the verse in Revelations 21:8 where John talks about *"the fearful and unbelieving…shall have their part in the lake which burneth."* If I followed the rules of the church to be a Christian, then would that give me confidence that I would avoid the lake of fire? If my church governs by the fear of punishment rather than love then as a member, I believe that is slavery.

Matthew 10:31 says, *"Fear you not therefore, you are of more value than many sparrows."* First Corinthians 6:23 says, *"For ye are bought with a price: therefore, glorify God in your body and in your spirit, which are God's."* He is always trying to dismantle my fearful way of thinking. Hebrews 4:16 says, *"Let us therefore come Boldly unto the throne of grace, that we may obtain mercy and find grace to help in time of need."*

As I grow closer to God, I am constantly learning what is healthy and unhealthy fear. Unhealthy fear is bondage. If what I am taught in the church does not free me to grow and be open to know more about who He is. Is it not the wrong fear? Wrong fear puts walls around me, fearing change. It freezes me from making decisions because it could be the wrong one. It is fear of stepping out of my familiar beliefs. Fear immobilizes me, not allowing the natural process to learn what is right and wrong. Could I trust God enough when I ask Him to show me the right way, especially when it does not agree with the way I was taught? Unhealthy fear is also putting down and judging others that do not believe the same as me.

Another kind of fear I had was an insecurity to express myself in conversations with friends or groups of people. I was taught that words were to be few and carefully considered before speaking. I was always evaluating if what I had to say was important. Questioning and hesitating took me inward to look at my worth. As an adult, this insecurity made me doubt that any input I had in most conversations were probably irrelevant. Was what I had to say important?

BEHIND THE SCENE

Was it right? My counselor asked me one day, "If you look at yourself, would you say that you are valuable?" It took me a long time to answer that question. What ran through my mind as I was searching for the right answer was, "If I say yes, then I could be seen as being proud." I knew that I was but the dust of the earth. What would he think of me if I gave the wrong answer? Will he approve? Would I be proud if I was valuable? I thought of the verse that said that we are *"fearfully and wonderfully made"* (Psalm 139:14 KJV). We are created in His image.

Suspicion. Suspicion is a cautious distrust. Suspicion is when someone expects the worst outcome to a problem. This can open a door for the worst to happen. When it does, that negative suspicion that was linked to your belief can then result in anger and criticism. I call that negative faith. When I have had the opportunity to listen to the details of their misfortune, I have found there are times when I hear a different answer to their dilemma. That is my opportunity to share other possibilities. When faith discerns with love and hope, I can then share what I see that God wants in the situation. Sometimes it is in hope where there is no hope.

I was plagued by the fear of failure. It made me defend what I did. *What if I fail,* I wondered, *how will that look?* If I keep looking back at my past decisions today, trying to perfect my choices, I will paralyze and disable my ability to make a new choice. I have heard it said, "If it is worth doing, then it is worth doing wrong." Wow! That is frightening. God forbid that I should do it wrong. I had to let go of expecting that everything should be perfect.

I heard my minister say one Sunday, "God cannot steer a parked car." In other words, keep moving. God will direct your path as you are in motion. Trust rids me of needing a sense of approval because my assurance is in God.

Shame. "Shame on you," was a term used frequently at home and in the community. Was there any good in me? How could I do it perfectly? As a child, how could I protect myself from shame when it is all about safety? It destroyed my ability to put value on what was important. I would always have to justify myself.

Shame ate at my soul and left me hopeless. When I worked long hours, I could get all the negative energy out from inside that would build up, but it was a cover. It was tough to sit still and take down the barricades and walls I had built from years of past hurts.

One of the manifestations of unhealthy shame is the fear of not belonging. Am I worth loving? Am I worth the risk of being loved? We deny the pain of not being loved by isolating ourselves and pushing it aside to avoid looking at it, all the while rejecting ourselves. In my shame from the incest, I became critical of my looks and rejected my body.

Sometimes when people lose self-worth, they find value by accomplishing works and doing conquests. They compare their value by using the actions of others to determine their worth. This is a roller coaster based on the actions of others. The religious mind rejects that in difficult times, God is completing what we are lacking in our life. When I accept and trust His kind intention toward me, I am free from defending and justifying. My question is this, "Is Christ dying enough for my sin, or does He need to put Himself back on the cross for the immensity of my sin to be forgiven?"

When I mess up, it brings out my limitations, which is an invitation to connect spirituality. God is working on my righteousness. He is not in the business of just correcting my sin. As I look at situations that turn me inward and depress me, I know without whitewashing any of it that this is also the beginning of my healing. My sadness is a part of my healing. It signals me of my limitations, which results in my desire to search for a deeper walk with God. Journaling has been a great way for me to write the depth of my wounds on paper that are difficult for me to express.

Healthy shame gives me the permission to be human. It is my conscience that signals the need to change when I mess up. It knows when something is wrong, confesses it, and moves on. As trust grows with this process, an emotional bond is formed, knowing He will do what He has promised. Jesus fulfilled the law by becoming sin for me. When God sees me, He sees Jesus's complete work.

My prayer is, "Lord, establish your worth through the finished work of Jesus and to experience Your love and peace that is beyond my wildest dreams."

Self-righteous. The Pharisees judged themselves as righteous by their own standards. That is a form of self-righteousness; however, that did not make them righteous. When the Lord says we are righteous and we in pride say we are unrighteous, that is parading as a false self-righteousness. The sin of self-righteousness was not the center focus but the fact that the Pharisees chose their own standards over God's. When I insist that my way is the only righteous way, I will never see nor experience God's incredible liberation of His righteousness in me. People can labor for a lifetime keeping painful memories pushed down, living by an outward standard of righteousness, and robbing them of experiencing the incredible liberation of God's righteousness by trying to earn it.

"As He is so are we in this world" (1 John 4:17 KJV). Under trials, the enemy would love to convince me that I have not changed. This is judging myself, which is destructive. Even while I make mistakes, when I am free of judgment and condemnation of myself and others, the world will see the love of God in me. He has a tough time shining through a rejected child. Change comes by hunger and exposure to the love of the Father.

Sometimes laws have a foundation of self-effort or works, which does not allow God or anyone to get close. This is the fear of being punished and rejected by God. This is an enemy of intimacy with God. It's not my knowledge of the word or the righteous following of rules that determines my identity with God but God's love for me in a relationship as a son or daughter.

As a believer, I know that God can do anything. But can or will He do it through me? I've heard believers say, "If it's His will." Is this an excuse then, if He does not do what I have prayed for? This is exalting my own self-limitation above the knowledge of God. This gives Satan access to limit Jesus's complete work that He wants to do. Sometimes when I don't know how to pray for someone, I ask the Lord to bind them to His will. I know my trust is not complete yet, but I keep opening my heart and saying, "Lord, I believe. Help my unbelief."

Salvation. When the verse was read to me in John 3:16, it was simple: *"For God so loved the world, that he gave His only begotten Son, that whosoever believeth in Him should not perish, but have eternal life."* I said I believe Him and invite Him into my heart.

The one who stands next to me now is Christ, my advocate. What He did on the cross was to give Himself and His blood that cleansed me. Now we no longer need to present the blood of goats as a sacrifice to God for our cleansing. When I take communion, which can be daily, I am remembering Him. I take His body and blood to become a new creation in Him. He breaks off the generational curses and changes my DNA.

One of my Amish friends said he was distraught as he heard it preached many times that he was a sinner with no solution given. I think this approach allows the Mennonites and Amish to evaluate their own worth about themselves. He concluded that the Amish teach salvation by obedience, and the Bible teaches salvation by faith.

My salvation is not based on how much knowledge of the Bible I have or how well I follow the rules. He daily sanctifies me. His grace frees me of a sin habit. His goodness and kindness are all around me, which changes me and allows me to ask for even more of Him.

Redemption. Redemption is not just to go to heaven but to have a deeper relationship with Him as the cycle of sin is broken for me and my children. As I went through the process of healing, remembering, and forgiving myself and my abusers, I had to give up old ways of protecting myself by allowing His redemption continually. Any attempt for me to work it out in my mind or make it okay on my part is in essence saying that what Christ did on the cross was not enough. No wonder the cross was too heavy for Him to carry.

Regret. What do I do with regrets? Do I punish myself because of my choices? Seventy times seven Jesus forgives me. In Leviticus 16, the Israelites had two goats. One was sacrificed for the Lord (their hearts and hands were cleansed when the blood was carried into the holy of holies), and the other was sent away as a scapegoat (their sins were put on the goat and sent into the wilderness). The Israelites were not allowed to do anything to warrant forgiveness. Christ did this for me by His spilt blood and taking our sin as the scapegoat and was crucified outside what was considered an unacceptable area for that day. I forgive myself and take myself off the judgment seat of my own rules that have failed to give salvation. I can write a new chapter for myself.

God doesn't see what is wrong with me. He looks at what is missing in my life and makes sure that what I go through is what I need to fill the areas that I lack. He is not just taking on the missing parts, such as anger or fear, but the parts that were added that do not belong. The cross was judgment for my sin once for all time.

The Bible talks about standing before the throne of God to be judged. Growing up in the church this fear was greatly emphasized. I now know God sent Jesus to hang on the cross as judgment for my sins. Today I stand next to my advocate Jesus. He is my judge. He is the one anointed to set me free. That is what judgment means to me. God loves the reflection of who Christ is in me.

One day when I was listening to a minister, he asked, "Are you looking to earn your salvation?" "Was Jesus punished enough for your sin?" If He wasn't punished enough because of my past, then my salvation is not complete. That would mean He needs to come back and suffer more because of my sin that I cannot forget or forgive. I do not want to nullify or put to nothing what He did. God, forgive me for thinking my sin is greater than His grace. He crucified my sin and is changing my sin nature and putting it to death. There is nothing that I could do that would make Him love me more or less because He is love.

Jesus. Jesus was always motivated by the kindness of His heart. He was always ministering to the disqualified and downcast. He healed those who could do nothing in return for Him. Because of this, we are challenged by God's goodness, not by the enemy's condemnation. Your freedom is learning how to be God-conscious. Sometimes when we forget, we make the problem larger than Him.

Jeremiah 22:16 says, *"He judged the cause of the poor and needy; then it was well with Him: was not this to know me? Saith the Lord."* Knowing who God is and learning what He is interested in has been so big for me. When I saw this verse, I was struck with the simplicity of it and how much the world needs this. It is to do something for someone who has not been able to achieve it. Amish and Mennonites are giving, kind, and, in my opinion, care about mankind.

Meekness. "*The meek shall inherit the earth.*" There are many interpretations on the meaning of *meekness*. I can tell you what it does not look like—the slumping of the shoulders or being beaten down, apologizing for who I am. It is not reserved, shy, subservient, or passive. There can be pride in doing the lowly jobs such as house cleaning. House cleaning is needed. I am not diminishing that if that is what you want. I have done it as a job, but it was not what I wanted to continue doing. I think if you want to become something outside of your family traditions and it requires more schooling to be able to accomplish it, it will be a source of fulfillment for you. God wants to give us the earth to rule. One of Adam's assignments was to rule the earth, and we are instructed to replenish it also. Meekness is to see God's promises in the Word, to know who I am by reminding God that what He says I believe. I may not know what that looks like, but it is my inheritance, but He says that the meek will inherit the earth.

Anger. "*Be angry and sin not,*" Ephesians 4:26 says. How does that look? I do not believe all anger is bad. Healthy anger is at an injustice that is done to yourself or others. God created us with emotions. I think anger is a good reaction when a wrong is suffered by hating the offense, especially when someone is wronged. It can be my strength to determine to change a situation.

Many survivors are afraid of tapping into their anger by expressing it. The fear of being misunderstood keeps them from talking, especially when the relationship between anger and love cannot coexist. Most of us at some time have been angry with those we love or are close to. For the abused, the positive experiences in childhood endangers the relationship when anger at a sibling or parent is expressed. I benefitted from the good experiences as a child, which gave me positive memories to hold onto. However, when I got angry at my past, I had no illusions of my abuser's innocence.

Survivors are also often afraid of expressing their anger because they feel like the depth of it will consume them. If they put words to it, they will fall into its depth of anger, being hateful, and even bitter with a possibility of not coming out of it. In one of the stages of my healing, I can say I was willing to do harm to my abusers; however, I found when anger is expressed and listened to by naming it, you no longer repress it or obsess on it, and the result is liberation.

The destructive side of anger that is a problem is the anger that criticizes, yells, and demeans another in the middle of a disagreement, especially when it destroys the opinion of others by attempting to make a point or attempting to control them. It can justify a wrong response toward another. A wrong in response to a wrong is not a solution.

Anger unexpressed and suppressed over time can be the source of bitterness, self-pity, and discouragement. Medically it has also been linked to cancer. That is why I believe it is vital to be able to discuss your anger to a person willing to listen objectively.

Relationships. Relationships are simply not always easy! If you have experienced incest, you should not be in a sexual relationship with someone who you cannot freely talk to. Why? Because that is a familiar pattern for you. When you cannot say no, then are you not sleeping with the perpetrator?

Here are some questions that are good to ask yourself when entering a relationship. Do I respect this person? Does this person respect me? Is this a person I can communicate with? Do we work through conflicts well? Do we both compromise? Is there give and take? Can I be honest? Am I able to reach my own goals? Is this person supportive of the changes I am trying to make and help me achieve them? To this day, there are times I look longingly at daughters that have a relationship to their dads, and I wish I had that in a loving earthly father.

Defensiveness. In my thirties, the realization hit me that in nearly all situations, I was defensive. Why? It protected me and pushed people away. I felt comfortable with in my aloneness. I was not open for anyone to correct me or tell me what to do, except occasionally my husband or at work. That is how I protected myself to try to keep control. I would not allow anyone too close in my life. I had to learn to slow down my response and remain open to retrain myself to learn what others intent was in the conversation.

Men and women. The kingdom of God is made up of people in relationship. Relationships I have found can be challenging. Men and women relate differently. Men want respect, especially as a provider of the family. They believe that this is an act of love. They also thrive on being told that they are respected for a job they did well. For a man, one of the tests of true authority and satisfaction is his willingness to serve by providing. This is not always understood by a wife who thrives on being told that she is loved.

For the woman, it is natural for them to give love. In return, they need to be told they are loved and look for it from their mate. It gives them value. I have heard men say, "Well, I told her a month ago that I love her." That is not enough. She needs to be told daily. Hug and cherish her. I read once that everyone needs at least four hugs a day.

Women want love and intimacy. If a woman's needs are not met, she sometimes manipulates to control a spouse, which is not loving. You have the right to withhold his sexual need, but it is not profitable. It is empowering to meet their needs. Honor him.

A husband has the responsibility to lay down his life for his wife, loving her. "*Husbands, love your wives. Just as Christ also loved the church*" (Ephesians 5:25 KJV). This is a huge responsibility for him. Ideally, the wife returns respect in response to his love.

Marriage is a partnership that requires working through difficult times. In the church world, I have listened to ministers teach that salvation for the wife comes through unconditional obedience to their husband. So why do I have a brain? This feels like slavery. I question whether this teaches me to love myself or place any value in my judgment. Of course, I can prefer him. But I want a relationship where there is respect with love for each other by coming to a decision by processing it together. When I as a woman have value, then I can return that value, which results in loving myself. The scripture says that I am to love my neighbor as myself. If I do not love myself, then can I completely love my neighbor or my husband?

There were times when I was not capable of having a good conversation with my husband. I went through what are called shame attacks. I could not look at people while in the middle of a conversation. I could not wait to get home to be alone. During these times, it seemed like all the negative thoughts from the gates of hell were yelling in my ear. When I exposed these lies to my husband, he would say, "No, this is a lie. This is not you." I would take what he said and claim that as my truth about myself. In this, he covered me by pointing me in the right direction.

Some churches have also taught that the man is the woman's covering. Is he my covering if Christ's love does not come through him? Christ as my Rabbi who has all authority is my covering, my teacher, my love. When Christ's love comes to me through my husband, then I know I can trust and return that love because I am reflecting Christ's love back to Him.

At first when disagreements happened between my husband and me, I did not know how to set boundaries. In my old religious mindset, I would have told myself that I needed to submit, which devaluates my opinion. I would give in to his wishes by not saying that I was uncomfortable with the decisions he made. Later I learned that it was much healthier to take the risk of being rejected by talking about what I believed. Now if my opinion differs, I am free to disagree. I am responsible first to my Heavenly Father, sharing with him what God has made real to me. Secondly, I am responsible to my husband by honoring him as I honor God, and together, we work it out. It is not him trying to make me into what he wants but encouraging me in my relationship with God, as we love each other, bringing out the best in the other.

I know some men like it when their wives obey without discussion, and I'm sorry if you are in that dilemma, but that is control, not love. We can disagree on issues but allow the other their opinion by honoring them. *"If two of you shall agree on earth as touching anything that they shall ask, it shall be done for them of my Father which is in heaven,"* Matthew 18:19 says. That is powerful.

Children. As a child growing up in a Mennonite family, it was important that I learn submission with obedience to authority. As an adult, my perspective on authority has taken on a much different interpretation. Authority to me is to encourage the spiritual growth of a child so they can find their own value. I believe the principles of it are essential to guide them to discover where their interests allow them to thrive.

Children mirror the parents' boundaries. One of the important parts of my life was to value my alone time. I understood that it is important to do the same for my children by respecting their solitary time to develop their own thoughts. This can be uncomfortable for parents who are concerned to have their children follow in their Christian beliefs. Alone time also allows them to develop emotional and thought boundaries. An important part of this is they have the right to say no to touch even if it is yours. I had to remind myself that it is about their development, not my offence when I was not needed, although I let them know that I was available when they needed me.

It is important for the child to be able to ask questions. It is important for them to form their own ideas and challenge existing beliefs. When the adult tells them how to think by not allowing questions, it makes it difficult for them to believe what is not real to them. By not interacting or denying their questions or allowing their own discovery is to close the door for any open discussion. If I shame the child for thinking another way, I have found they close down and withhold what they are thinking. They can no longer share their thoughts or ask questions. *"A soft answer turneth away wrath: but grievous words stir up anger"* (Proverbs 15:1 KJV). For my children, I want them to ask questions for discussion. Let's stay open and find answers together. I don't think God dislikes questions. I'm not talking here about discipline for bad behavior.

My obedience to the rules of the church and God was driven by a lot of fear. Today I know that love destroys fear. There did not seem to be enough of that to go around. If there is no love, then discipline is by fear. As I got older, obedience to the rules of the church was expected as the Bible was interpreted by leadership. If I did not follow and repent, my destination would be hell. If I obeyed, I could hope to go to heaven unless there was something God found wrong with me on judgment day. Now that to me is fear! In Revelations 21:8, John talks about the fearful and unbelieving being the first to go to the lake of fire. If I followed the rules of the church to be a Christian, then would that give me the confidence that I would avoid the lake of fire, or was there always a fear that I could be doing it wrong and He would send me there anyway?

The church and "the world."

We have made our own world or church system based on how we have been raised, and we've placed ourselves in the center as the ruler. In the kingdom of God, it is our relationship with Him and each other that gives us the wisdom to make the right decisions every day that is free from my kingdom or the world's kingdom. In John 14 and 15, His last words with the apostles were to love even if it is not returned. This to me is what it means to be a part of His kingdom and not a part of the world.

What does it mean to not be like "the world" that the Bible refers to so many times? It does not mean God's creation that is circulating around in space. It is referring to the world's systems that operate on evil premises such as self-centeredness, fear, greed, control, power, and deceit often found in the political arenas. John said, *"For God so loved the world."* Matthew said in the Lord's prayer, *"Thy Kingdom come on earth as it is in heaven."* He loves His creation.

CHAPTER 17

Sometimes when I learn new things in the Bible, I want to share it with everyone. I find there are times that others are not as excited, or they disagree with my observation. I try not to become defensive because that makes me protective of what I have learned in the scripture. Should I insist that my way is the only way to look at it, then that closes the door for me to continue to learn more. That could make me judgmental and self-righteous. So please allow me to share and keep discovering.

In the following subjects below, I cover subjects that are not related to the original intent of this book, but these subjects are gems of what I have learned through the years and wanted to share. Some of the subjects I am still learning and grappling with.

1. God originally created Satan as the reflection of Himself. His name was Lucifer (Luciferous), which is the illuminated one or light bearer. He wore a breastplate of stones that reflected God's glory when he came into God's presence. He must have been beautiful when all the colors shone by a reflection of God. For example, a diamond stone in the sun reflects beautiful colors. That is why he was called Lucifer. He had to remove his shining breastplate when he rebelled against God and was thrown out of heaven. He was then called Satan.

2. Christ said to His followers, *"For my Yoke is easy, and my burden is lite"* (Matthew 11:30). I did not understand why He compared his yoke to the yoke of an ox as being easy. A strong ox pulls with the yoke on his shoulders the weight that is behind him. Then I learned more about what the yoke meant in that day.

    Every Jewish boy memorized the Torah from Genesis to Deuteronomy in the hopes of becoming a rabbi. When they were questioned in the temple by the teachers, it was not just to recite what they had memorized but their ability to ask questions and discuss the content, which gave insight into the Word. Remember at twelve years old, when Joseph and Mary accidentally left Jesus at the temple? When His parents found Him, the Pharisees were amazed that He was so well learned.

    Later they said of Him, *"He is one with authority,"* and they called Him *rabbi*. He challenged every prior rabbi's tradition and teaching because He was allowed to do that as a rabbi.

    The schooling in that day went from age twelve to thirty. The students who wanted to be a rabbi and failed went back to their family trade. So when Christ called to the fisherman to follow Him, they left it all. Did you ever wonder why they were so willing? Because every Jewish boy wanted to be a rabbi. When they were disqualified in rabbi school, they longed to hear the words from a rabbi with authority to say those words: *"Follow me."* It was no accident that He chose the rejected.

3. When they brought the woman caught in adultery to Him to test Him, they said the law says that you must stone one that is caught in the act. The requirement was for two witnesses who were not guilty of sin to stone. Jesus said, *"He that is without sin among you, let him first cast a stone at her"* (John 8:7 KJV). *"Woman, where are those thine accusers? hath no man condemned thee? She said, No man, Lord.*

And Jesus said unto her, Neither do I condemn thee: go and sin no more" (John 8:10–11 KJV). His yoke is easy.

4. The Bible is given to us and is the inspired word of God. (Inspired means to breathe in). It has more than forty authors. And as I look at the changes from Genesis to Revelation, I see that God doesn't change, but He continues to change us, and it keeps getting better. An example of this was Abraham when he took Isaac to sacrifice him. Child sacrifice was a religious tradition that was handed down from his father. An angel stopped his hand, and God supplied a goat in the thicket for Abraham to sacrifice. From then, animals were sacrificed instead of children. Was it the perfect answer? No, but it was an improvement. When Christ came, He was the ultimate sacrifice.
5. Another area that some denominations have taken seriously by making it a tradition is where Paul in 1 Corinthians 11 writes to the Corinthians to instruct the women to cover their heads. This passage seems to be the only one where these instructions are given. This is and has been an important part of the church.

The government at that time where the church of Corinth was, was ruled by the Romans. Their aggressive ways could snatch a woman off the street and rape her, which they did at will. If she was wearing a veil, it meant she was spoken for. So for this reason, Paul instructed the young girls to cover their heads, especially when praying or prophesying in public, which was to protect them.

Acts 21:9 says, *"And the same man had four daughters, virgins, which did prophesy."* It doesn't say if they had their heads covered because they were virgins.

In the Old Testament, when they went to battle, they would kill all, including women and children. Deuteronomy 21:10–12 changed that.

When thou goest forth to war against thine enemies, and the Lord thy God hath delivered them into thine hands and thou hast taken them captive, And seest among the captives a beautiful woman, and hast a desire unto her, that thou wouldest have her to thy wife; Then thou shalt bring her home to thine house; and she shall shave her head and pare [which is to cut] her nails.

In that day, it was an honor to be spared from battle and taken in as a wife. It was not a shame to have her head shaven and her nails clipped. It wasn't the final solution, but it was an improvement over getting killed by their captors.

When my husband and I were traveling to Israel, I noticed that many of the married women wore wigs that were styled in a short stylish haircut. This was a way to cover their heads. I did not speak to any of them to inquire, but perhaps there is some indication that a woman should cover her head. Some of the other orthodox women wore veils.

CHAPTER 18

*T*he Kingdom of God. Christ spoke many times of the kingdom of God. He mentioned it more often than He spoke of the church. Luke 17:20–21 records that *"the kingdom of God cometh not with observation: neither shall they say, lo here! or, lo there!"* The kingdom of God is not coming to be observed in others or an organization necessarily, but he goes on to say, *"For, behold, the kingdom of God is within you."* The word *within* in the original Hebrew language means inside of your very being or in the midst of your body. This is the kingdom of light within us that our eyes see which guide us. Christ referred to the blindness of men's hearts on various occasions. He is the light that keeps no record of wrong.

One of our biggest challenges is that we do not see who we truly are. My spirit communes with God. We are spirit beings in a human body with a soul. God reminds us to come back to our purpose of who He has called us to be. He longs for us to be mature as His sons and daughters. It's the prodigal son whom the father rushes out to give a kiss, puts a ring on his son's finger, and covers him with his robe. His love allows me to go beyond where I ever thought I could go.

I like to remind God of who He is in me. I take a promise He gives in the Bible and put it on a piece of paper and hang it on the wall. Every day when I look at it, I speak it out loud, or I can yell it quietly on the inside of me reminding God that I know what He promised.

BEHIND THE SCENE

One of my letters to God

Dear God,

I am embraced by You, consumed by your love, God for me. When circumstances are resistant, your favor shows me through. What is it, Lord, that you want to be to me today that you were not able to be yesterday? Put me in your favor. Let me sing of you. Let me dance with you. Fill me to all Your fullness.

Please change my heart. I know, with you, it's all possible. I know you can heal me and especially the pain of my past. I am so sad. You have already helped me concerning my defensiveness. Trying to protect myself when I feel attacked. Now I am opening up, not reacting by trying to cover up. After all, it could be something about them. It's not all about me.

Come into my heart of hearts and love me unconditionally. Be my love, my Daddy. Commune with me. Tell me I'm beautiful. Tell me I'm eternal. Tell me who I am. I don't know what that means or how that looks. I just know I want it. I know everything is for a purpose. Nothing just happens.

Love,
Me

REFERENCES

How to Stop the Pain by Dr James B. Richards
The Courage to Heal by Ellen Bass and Laura Davis
Forgiveness by Maureen Burns
Shane Willard, shanewillardministries.org
Graham Cooke, brilliantperspective.com
Barbara Lepsen, upwardscounseling.com (919-455-5858)

ABOUT THE AUTHOR

Marianne is the sixth of seven children. Life on the farm was structured with many responsibilities at an early age. Education was discouraged. At fifteen, she worked as an aide in a nursing home, which confirmed her desire to become a nurse. Her nursing education began in Michigan and was completed in Los Angeles as a registered nurse. She is married and has four children and six grandchildren. After twenty-seven years in emergency nursing, she could see how patients would benefit by having support to do life differently. She began taking courses on how to help others heal body, soul, and spirit, which she taught in a few churches and small groups. When her husband retired, they moved to the foothills of the beautiful Blue Ridge Mountains in North Carolina; and occasionally, they visit what she calls God's great pond, the ocean. Her life is busy with children, grandchildren, friends, and church.

If you would like to connect to get help with what the contents of the book are about, please contact behindthescene.marianne@yahoo.com.